PRAISE FOR *The Automat*

"[Bach's] cheery, can-do message . . . cuts through
challenge of buying a house for the first-timer. . . . For a newcomer,
it's fundamental reading."

—*USA Today*

"A great book that first-time homeowners and anyone toying with
the notion of investing in real estate will find immensely practical .
. . Bach offers universally good advice on how to begin saving and
guiding wealth through homeownership. . . . Wildly motivational."

—*Publishers Weekly* (starred review)

"If you read only one real estate book this year, it should be *The
Automatic Millionaire Homeowner*. . . . This is one of the few real
estate books that cannot be recommended too highly for both
beginner and experienced homeowners."

—Robert J. Bruss, *Miami Herald*

PRAISE FOR *The Automatic Millionaire*

"*The Automatic Millionaire* is an automatic winner. David Bach really cares about you: on every page you can hear him cheering you on to financial fitness. No matter who you are or what your income is, you can benefit from this easy-to-apply program. Do it now. You and your loved ones deserve big bucks!"

—Ken Blanchard, coauthor of *The One Minute Manager*®

"*The Automatic Millionaire* gives you, step-by-step, everything you need to secure your financial future. When you do it David Bach's way, failure is not an option."

—Jean Chatzky, Financial Editor, NBC's *Today*

"David Bach's no-spin financial advice is beautiful because it's so simple. If becoming self-sufficient is important to you, then this book is a must."

—Bill O'Reilly, anchor, *Fox News*, and author of
The O'Reilly Factor and *The No Spin Zone*

"Finally, a book that helps you stop sweating it when it comes to your money! *The Automatic Millionaire* is a fast, easy read that gets you to take action. David Bach is the money coach to trust year in and year out to motivate you financially."

—Richard Carlson, author of *Don't Sweat the Small Stuff*

THE AUTOMATIC
MILLIONAIRE HOMEOWNER™

Also by David Bach

Start Late, Finish Rich

The Automatic Millionaire®

The Automatic Millionaire Workbook

The Finish Rich Workbook

Smart Couples Finish Rich®

Smart Women Finish Rich®

1001 Financial Words You Need to Know

THE

AUTOMATIC

MILLIONAIRE

HOMEOWNER™

*A Powerful Plan to
Finish Rich in Real Estate*

CANADIAN EDITION

DAVID BACH

 DOUBLEDAY CANADA

THE AUTOMATIC MILLIONAIRE HOMEOWNER. Copyright © 2006 David Bach.

Paperback edition 2008

The Automatic Millionaire Homeowner, The Automatic Millionaire, The Latte Factor, DOLP, Smart Women Finish Rich, Smart Couples Finish Rich are registered trademarks of FinishRich, Inc.

Doubleday Canada and colophon are trademarks.

Library and Archives Canada Cataloguing in Publication applied for.

ISBN: 978-0-385-66175-1

Printed and bound in the USA

Published in Canada by
Doubleday Canada, a division of
Random House of Canada Limited

Visit Random House of Canada Limited's website: www.randomhouse.ca

BVG 10 9 8 7 6 5 4 3 2 1

To the millions of readers of the
FinishRich books and *The Automatic Millionaire:*
Thank you for your feedback, your encouragement,
your letters and e-mails, and your success stories.
You inspire me and our team at
FinishRich Media to do what we do.

CONTENTS

PREFACE TO THE
PAPERBACK EDITION

You hold in your hands a simple, easy-to-read book that can change your life. *The Automatic Millionaire Homeowner* is not a get-rich-quick book. It is based on proven, timeless concepts and offers a realistic approach to real estate that has helped real people achieve real success.

My mission in writing it was to inspire those of you who are renters to go out and buy your own home. Why? Because over the last two decades as a financial advisor, financial coach, and author, I have seen firsthand that nothing will change your financial future faster than owning your own home. Homeownership is the foundation on which almost all wealth is built, and it can be the foundation on which you and those you love become financially free.

In recent months, the newspapers have been filled with negative news about real estate. But the fact is that home-ownership is still a great long-term investment.

This book, the seventh in the FinishRich Series, was originally published in 2006. It was an instant national bestseller in both the United States and Canada, reaching the top of the *New York Times, Wall Street Journal, USA Today,* and *Business-Week* bestseller lists. As part of the launch, I toured thirteen cities across America and kicked off a financial literacy initiative that I called the *Great American Homeowner Challenge(tm).* This initiative, which was sponsored by Wells Fargo, was designed to inspire tenants to become homeowners—and homeowners to build wealth by buying a second home or investment property. In a matter of weeks, I had the pleasure of appearing before more than thirty thousand people at our free seminars, and all who attended received a free copy of this book. As part of The Great American Homeowner Challenge, we held an essay contest and awarded the winner $250,000 (after taxes) towards the purchase of a home. You'll read the winning essay in our success story chapter. I also donated more than $175,000 to Habitat for Humanity to help them offer those in need a chance at the dream of homeownership.

Although there are already more than a million copies of this book in print, its mission is not complete. So, for this paperback edition, we've updated all the facts and figures and left the core message intact. We've also added a new chapter of success stories, which features a selection of inspiring true tales culled from the thousands of letters and emails we've received from readers since *The Automatic Millionaire Homeowner* first came out. Reading these stories, you can learn how real people like you have changed their lives financially and realized their dreams of homeownership. If they can do it, so can you. The dream of homeownership can and should be yours.

I hope this book helps you. Let me know if it does, because your stories inspire us to continue doing what we do. Thank you for reading. Enjoy . . . and Live Rich!

DAVID BACH
New York
August 2007

INTRODUCTION

What if I told you the smartest investment you would ever make during your lifetime would be a home?

What if I told you that the way in which you buy your homes over the course of your lifetime would determine whether you ever become rich?

What if I told you that in just an hour or two I could share with you a simple system that would help you become rich through homeownership?

What if I told you that this system was called the Automatic Millionaire Homeowner—and that if you spent an hour or two with me, you could learn how to become one?

Would you be interested? Would you be willing to spend a few hours with me? Would you like to become an Automatic Millionaire Homeowner?

—DAVID BACH

If the lines above got your attention, then please keep reading. Stay where you are for a few minutes and read just a few more pages. Whether you rent or own, this book can transform your life. It's a powerfully simple plan—a lifelong strategy for wealth building that works in any market because it's based on time-tested wisdom that is tried and true.

CANADIANS ARE STAYING
CLOSER TO HOME!

Over the last few years, something radical happened to the way Canadians think about money and investing—something so radical that it may have forever changed the way we live our lives and plan for our futures. What happened is that a lot of people got fed up with the stock market.

The reason for this change of heart was simple. Between August 2000 and September 2002, Canadian stocks experienced their worst decline since the Depression in 1929–1932. After a bull market that began in 1998, Canadian stocks lost 43 percent of their value between the summer of 2000 and the fall of 2002. To say the least, it was one brutal meltdown. Even though the Canadian stock market in general and technology stocks in particular bounced back by 2004, the effects of the meltdown linger to this day.

For many families—maybe yours was one of them—this market "correction" (which is what the experts called it) was the proverbial straw that broke the camel's back. Canadians simply decided that enough was enough. They were taking their stock market "chips" and going home—literally and figuratively.

Instead of keeping their money in stocks, many Canadians started investing in real estate—mainly in homes, home improvements, and second homes. This simple change has led to a boom in real estate and homeownership the likes of which we've seldom seen before. It's an exciting time to be building wealth in Canada, but it's also a frightening time because Canadians now have so much of their wealth tied up in their homes—about $1.6 trillion in equity, according to Statistics Canada, or about 77 percent of non-financial assets. According to a report from Scotiabank, the value of real estate assets in Canada rose by 27 percent between 2002 and 2005, more than double the 13 percent increase in household financial assets. Home equity now accounts for 36 percent of the average net worth of homeowner households in Canada, up from 29 percent in 2000.

And many people are wondering—maybe you're one of them—whether this is a safe place to be.

SMART HOMEOWNERS ARE FINISHING RICH—HOW ABOUT YOU?

Between 1997 and 2006, the average Canadian homeowner saw the value of his house jump by almost 50 percent. Since 1980, according to The Canadian Real Estatxe Association, the average Canadian home has increased in value by more than 200 percent. Many homeowners doubled or even tripled their wealth in just a few years because of exploding real estate values. As prices soared, experts began warning that the real estate market was starting to look like the overheated technology market of the late 1990s. Nonetheless, as I write, the gold rush to real estate continues.

The average home price in Canada hit $237,900 in 2005—up $15,000 from $224,729 the year before. Not as high as increases in the U.S., but that was just the average. In some markets, including Edmonton and Calgary, home prices have risen more than 8 percent in the same period. In Vancouver, the average price of a house is $400,000. Some people have literally bought a home, lived in it for a few years, then sold it and retired. Done. Game over.

Imagine that. Buy a home, live in it, build your wealth—and then retire rich. It may sound too good to be true. But it's not. It has happened—and it will continue to happen for thousands of people over the next few decades. The question is, will it happen for you? Will you catch this wave, miss it—or will it crash on you?

BOOM OR BUST—YOU CAN STILL MAKE MONEY IN REAL ESTATE

As I sit here in August 2005, I have no idea when you will be reading what I'm writing. Maybe it's March 2006 (when this book is scheduled to be published)—by which time the real estate market could be slowing or cooling down to more modest annual gains (or not). Perhaps this book was bought by a friend of yours who passed it along to you—and it's now 2007 and those once "certain" boom markets are going bust because of speculation. Or maybe the opposite has happened—interest rates have remained at historic lows, and home prices have continued their march upwards.

In fact, it doesn't really matter when you happen to be reading this or what's going on right now in the markets. This book is not about the boom . . . or the busts. It's not about timing the real estate market. It's not about the fantasy of "getting rich overnight" in real estate.

What this book is about is the truth. And the truth is this:

Nothing you will ever do in your lifetime
is likely to make you as much money as
buying a home and living in it.

Realistically, the best investment you will ever make will be your home.

Don't worry about timing the market in real estate. It's time *in* the market that will matter for you.

HOMEOWNERS GET RICH
AND TENANTS STAY POOR

The bottom line is this: the Canadian ambition of building a nest egg by owning a home is no fantasy. Homeowners have been getting rich off their real estate for years, and they will continue to do so in the future. There are also more of them than ever before. In fact, as I write this, more than 7 million Canadian householders—67 percent of Canadian families— own their own home, according to government statistics, up from less than 63 percent in 1991. And it's not just wealthy people who are buying homes. More people under the age of twenty-five are buying homes than ever before.

The same thing is happening all over the world. According to a report in the *Economist* magazine, the total value of residential property in developed countries has soared in recent years, rising from $40 trillion to $70 trillion. The fact is, never before have so many people in so many countries seen housing prices rise so much for so long.

So if owning a home is working so well, what's not working? The first answer is renting. For tentants, the facts are frankly a little depressing.

IF YOU WANT TO BE RICH, DON'T RENT

I apologize up front if you're a renter, because I know this may be brutal to hear, but you have to hear it if you're going to change. So here goes.

You simply can't get rich renting. We know this. It's a timeless truth. As Canada Mortgage and Housing Corporation (CMHC) points out, the net worth of homeowners has increased since 1984 far more rapidly than the net worth of tenants.

Try this on for size:

Between 1984 and 1999, the income and wealth of Canada's homeowners increased dramatically and that of tenants decreased, according to the Centre for Urban and Community Studies at the University of Toronto. Homeowners' wealth increased from being twenty-nine times that of tenants in 1984 to seventy times that of tenants in 1999.

Homeowners' wealth surpassed $140,000, while the wealth of non-owners fell to about $2,000.

The comparison is pretty stunning.

Could it be any clearer?

The point is that if you're renting, it's time to stop. Not that there's anything wrong with people who rent. Tenants aren't bad people. In fact, my goal for you is to someday own some homes or condos that you can rent to other people. It's just that if you are a tenant yourself, I don't want you to continue being one much longer.

LET'S TAKE A JOURNEY TOGETHER— AND SEE HOW EASY THIS CAN BE

This book is the eighth one I've written in the FinishRich Series; as of this writing, there are more than 5 million copies of these books in print, translated into 15 languages. If this is the first FinishRich book you've obtained, let me start by saying "thank you" for the opportunity to be your money guide and coach. If you are a returning reader, let me say a sincere "thank you" for your trust in me.

Writing these books has been an amazing journey for me. Each and every day, my team and I at FinishRich Media receive letters and e-mails from readers sharing with us how they've taken to heart the messages and lessons they've read in my books and used them to change their lives for the better.

WHY THIS BOOK NOW?

Back in January of 2004, I published a little book called *The Automatic Millionaire*, which immediately became a #1 *New York Times* and international bestseller. That month, I also had the incredible opportunity to share my book's simple message on *The Oprah Winfrey Show*. Our goal on *Oprah* was to teach millions of viewers how easy it could be to become an Automatic Millionaire by "paying yourself first" and making all your savings automatic. No budget was needed, no discipline was required. All it would take to achieve real wealth over your lifetime was a simple program that anyone could set up in an hour.

One section of *The Automatic Millionaire*—and also one of my appearances on *Oprah*—focused on real estate, making the point that after "paying yourself first," the most important thing you could do to achieve wealth was to buy a home. This prompted literally tens of thousands of readers to ask me the same question: "But how do I buy a home?" Others wrote, "I own a home but I don't feel rich. How do I use my home to become a millionaire?"

That's why I wrote this book.

MY MISSION WITH THIS BOOK IS TO HELP YOU USE HOMEOWNERSHIP TO BUILD REAL WEALTH FOR LIFE— AUTOMATICALLY!

For many of our parents and grandparents, real estate is a safety net. The equity in their houses is the cushion that supports them financially during retirement.

But I have a different—and better—plan for you. *Automatic Millionaire Homeowners are proactive.* They look at their homes not just as potential safety nets but as the means to live and get rich. That's my goal for you.

My mission with this book is to show you how homeownership can be the centrepiece of your wealth-building strategy, the key to achieving financial independence. Like *The Automatic Millionaire,* this book is designed to be read in just a few hours. In the process, you will learn everything you need to know, quickly and simply, to become an Automatic Millionaire Homeowner.

If you don't already own a home, I will take you by the hand and lead you step-by-step through the process of going from renting to homeownership. And once you become a homeowner—or if you already are one—I'll show you how to use your property to build wealth. Remember, when you purchase a home you're doing more than just buying a place to live. You're creating an opportunity for true financial independence. If done properly, homeownership can be a foundation on which you can build real wealth—even if you never earn more than an ordinary income. Real estate has always been the leading tool people have used to build wealth in Canada—and it is not too late for it to work for you.

Most important, I'm going to share with you how to make your home-buying experience as "automatic" as possible. In particular, I'll show you how to automate your mortgage payments so you can build equity in your home faster—increasing your net worth and opening a whole new world of possibilities for you. Ultimately, this little trick will enable you to become debt free years ahead of schedule—which could save you tens of thousands of dollars in mortgage interest and possibly even help you retire five to ten years early.

IT'S NEVER TOO LATE TO CATCH THE REAL ESTATE WAVE

"But, David, are you sure it's not too late?"

As I've travelled around the world in recent years doing television and radio shows, seminars, readings, and book signings, I've had the honor of meeting tens of thousands of readers. And at every event, speech and airport encounter, I get asked the same questions. "David, what about real estate?" "Is it too late for me?" "Can I still buy a home?" "What type of mortgage should I use?" "What about buying a second home?" "My friend is investing in condos and flipping them. What do you think about that? "My home has doubled in value in the last five years. Should I sell it and cash out?"

In fact, well over half the questions I get these days are about real estate. Given the sterling performance of the real estate market over the last few years, this really isn't very surprising. Nonetheless, the questions remain.

Is it too late for you to catch this real estate wave? Or, as was the case with the stock market in the late 1990s, are we experiencing a bubble that's about to pop?

The answers to these questions will be found in this book. But I can tell you one thing right now: There's no reason to worry that homeownership will turn out to have been nothing more than a passing fad. And here's why:

AS LONG AS YOU'RE ALIVE, YOU HAVE TO LIVE SOMEWHERE

Read that again. *"As long as you're alive, you have to live somewhere."*

This is one of those facts of life that's so obvious we don't even think about it. Everybody has to live somewhere, and someone owns every place where someone lives. It may be your parents, or a landlord, or the government—but someone has owned every place where you and every one of your neighbours have lived.

Why shouldn't that someone be you?

HOW THIS BOOK WORKS

Every time the real estate markets take off, publishers pump out what seems like thousands of books and tapes on "how to get rich in real estate." Chances are, you've bought some of these books or tapes yourself. I know I have. Some of them are truly inspiring, but few of them give you a real plan. They say you should own real estate if you want to be rich—but they don't tell you how. And many of them advocate unrealistic schemes that take so much work you'd practically have to quit your day job to put them into practice.

If you've read any of my other books in the FinishRich Series™, you know I don't do that. I want to inspire you to act, but I also want you to know and understand *exactly* what you need to do. And I make it simple—simple enough for you to be able to act quickly.

My books are about taking action—because it's action that ultimately will change your life.

So let's get started on our journey.

First, you're going to meet the "original" Automatic Millionaire Homeowner. In my years of being a financial advisor, author, and speaker, I've actually met thousands of Automatic Millionaire Homeowners. In fact, I've met more people who have become rich through real estate and homeownership than through any other means.

Lately, of course, it's become hard to avoid people who like to brag about the money they've made in real estate. In fact, it's often the main topic of conversation at cocktail parties, and to me that's worrisome. The people you hear bragging about buying and "flipping" properties are just like the folks who bragged about their "dot-com" stocks in the late 1990s. Many of them are probably over leveraged and are bound to get hurt financially. Some will lose their homes to foreclosure and, worse, may even end up bankrupt.

This book is not about how to be like those people. In fact, it's the opposite. It's about how to keep from getting sucked into the "buzz of a boom" and making foolish decisions—in short, how to become an Automatic Millionaire Homeowner who builds real wealth through a lifetime of homeownership.

These "average" homeowner millionaires are all around you, and there is no reason you can't become one yourself. John and Lucy Martin, whom you're going to meet in the first chapter, are just such a success story. I met them about ten years ago and through their example realized how simple homeownership can make anyone rich—if you have a plan to make it happen.

The Martins' story did more than educate me. It inspired me to take action, to try to do what they had done. As a result, in just ten years I've increased my net worth by more than $1 million simply through home buying.

Not bad considering I've only bought three homes so far in my life. So read their story and let it sink in. It's designed to open up your thinking—and inspire you to become an Automatic Millionaire Homeowner yourself. In the ten chapters that follow the Martins' story, I'll give you step-by-step instructions on exactly how to put yourself on the path to riches they took, teaching you how to transform yourself from a tenant to a homeowner—and from a homeowner to an *Automatic Millionaire Homeowner.*

YOU DON'T HAVE TO
DO THIS YOURSELF

From the outside, the real estate game can seem complicated and competitive, filled with lots of players, all of whom are striving to win. Because of this, many people simply give up on being a homeowner. Or if they become a homeowner, they never take the next step and buy a second home or a rental property.

My goal with this book is to show you how easy it can be to find your way through this seemingly complicated world. I'll explain what all these players really do and teach you how to pick good ones who can help you on your journey to becoming an Automatic Millionaire Homeowner. I'll translate the jargon real estate professionals use. Once you speak their language—and know what questions to ask—none of it will seem so intimidating.

ALMOST ANYONE CAN
BUY A HOME TODAY

You may think that if you've got a bad credit record, a lot of credit card debt, or not enough cash for a down payment, there's no way you could buy a home. If so, you'd be wrong.

In fact, you wouldn't believe how easy it is for almost anyone to buy a home today, especially first-time homebuyers. There are programs set up specifically to help people who have no money for a down payment. There are national banks that will loan you more than 100 percent of the cost of a home. And there are institutions that will structure loans so that your monthly mortgage payment will be the same as the rent you may be paying right now.

If any of this seems confusing—or too good to be true—*don't worry.*

The fact is that home buying is both easier and more straightforward than most people realize. Not only do both the government and the banks want you to become a homeowner, but thanks to the Internet you can shop for a loan, find a real estate agent, and search for available properties without ever leaving your couch. And in this book, I'll show you how to do it all.

THE PHILOSOPHY BEHIND THE AUTOMATIC MILLIONAIRE HOMEOWNER

- You can't get rich renting.
- You don't need a lot of money for a down payment on a home.
- You don't need good credit to buy a home.
- You should buy a home even if you have credit card debt.

- By adopting what I call the "Automatic Millionaire Mindset," you can build a fortune by buying just a few homes over the course of a lifetime.
- Homeowners get rich; landlords get *really* rich.
- *Above all, you need an "automatic system" to keep your real estate plan on track and guarantee that you won't fail.*

To make things even easier, this book is more interactive than any I've ever written. Each chapter ends with a short summary outline I call the Automatic Millionaire Homeowner Action Steps. These steps are your "ready, set, go" exercises—point-by-point instructions that you can use to make progress quickly towards your dream of homeownership and becoming an Automatic Millionaire Homeowner.

So let's get started. Let's take a look at how John and Lucy Martin became Automatic Millionaire Homeowners, and then let's go look at how you can do the same.

In just a few hours, I believe you'll be surprised by how much your thinking can change. And as your thinking changes, you'll begin to see—as thousands of people already have—that you can do it, too.

FREE! AUTOMATIC MILLIONAIRE SEMINAR—IN CANADA

Each book I write contains a gift. It's my way of saying "thank you" for allowing me to become your money coach. On the Automatic Millionaire website at **www. finishrich.com** you'll find an audio of one of my Automatic Millionaire Seminars, recorded in front of a live audience in Toronto of 7,000 people. You can download it or listen to the seminar online. Have fun listening!

CHAPTER ONE

MEETING THE AUTOMATIC MILLIONAIRE HOMEOWNER

I'll never forget when I met my first Automatic Millionaire Homeowner. I was in my late twenties and was on one of my first book tours, giving a talk at a bookstore in San Jose, California.

After a long down period, the real estate market in California was starting to take off and many of the people who had come to see me had questions about whether now was a good time to buy property. In the middle of discussing the benefits of homeownership, I called on a young woman named Karen, who seemed particularly agitated. "David," she asked, "what do you think of selling your house and buying another one so you can flip it to make a quick profit?"

I told Karen that I didn't agree with flipping properties. "What type of real estate do you own?" I said.

Karen blushed a little, then said, "Actually, I don't own any yet, but I just read a book on real estate that said I could make money flipping condo properties. She shrugged helplessly. "It all sounded so tempting. I'm not sure where to start."

"We'll let me ask you something else," I replied. "Do you have a lot of assets right now?"

Karen shook her head. "Not really."

I smiled at her. "You just read a book on real estate," I said. "Why? Is it flipping real estate that matters to you or the financial freedom you're hoping to get from it?"

"The financial freedom," Karen said firmly. "I want to get out of debt, stop renting, and finally get ahead. I'm tired of living paycheque to paycheque."

"That's great. Congratulations on knowing what you want and making a decision to get there. You've already done the hard part—something that most people never do. Now, how about we focus on it one step at a time? Instead of worrying about whether or not you can make a lot of money in a short period, let's look at how you would go from renting to home-ownership. That's really your first step in building assets."

Karen nodded enthusiastically. "I know," she said. "My parents told me that I should focus on buying a home. The book I read said I should look at foreclosures and buy real estate with no money down. But the book didn't really explain how to do it. It just said rich people do this all the time."

LEARNING FROM THE
REAL WORLD OF REAL PEOPLE

I knew the book Karen was talking about. At the time, it was very popular and I had read it myself. It contained some valuable ideas and information, so I didn't want to single it out. Instead, I looked around at the audience and asked, "How many of you have seen one of those 'No Money Down' real estate infomercials?

There were more than 100 people in the room and pretty much all of them raised their hands.

"Great," I said. "Now, how many of you have actually bought a property with no money down?"

Out of the 100 people there, two raised their hands.

"OK, so we know it's not impossible to buy real estate with no money down. But we also know it's not very common, nor is it necessarily easy.

"Here's another question for you. How many of you own your own homes or condos?"

About half the audience raised their hands.

"For those of you who own a home or condo, keep your hand up if it's the best investment you ever made."

Nearly every hand that was already up stayed up.

"OK, keep your hands up and let me put a question to the rest of you who don't own your own homes. How many of you have had your parents or grandparents tell you that their home was their best investment they ever made?"

Now, nearly EVERY single hand in the room was raised.

"Isn't that interesting?" I said. "What we just did was conduct a real-life test on real people about what seems to work in the real world. And you know what we've learned? We've learned that there's a lot of 'razzle-dazzle' out there in real estate. 'Buy real estate with no money down.' It's not that you can't do something like that. But that's not what you should be focusing on.

"What we've just seen is that there is one thing that is being done over and over again that works like a charm consistently—and that is buying a home and owning it for a while."

I turned back to Karen, who smiled and laughed. "Okay, I get it," she said. "Stop renting and buy a home! That seems to make a lot of sense. Now if you could just help me with the down payment, I'd be all set."

The audience laughed.

"I've got a better idea," I said, laughing along with them. "How about I teach you how to save up the money you'll need for a down payment and how to get the financing you'll need from the bank. The truth is that there are many special loan programs for first-time homebuyers that can help you buy a place faster than you'd think."

Karen's smile widened. "Sounds good to me!" she said.

THE MOST IMPORTANT INVESTMENT YOU WILL EVER MAKE IS YOUR HOME

As Karen sat down, I caught sight of an older couple I had spotted earlier in the back of the room. They were sitting there with their arms crossed. When you're speaking to an audience, crossed arms are usually a bad sign, but these two folks were both nodding and smiling.

After the question-and-answer session ended, I spent twenty minutes or so signing copies of my book. To my surprise, I noticed the older couple patiently waiting for me to finish. When I finally did, they came up to me. "David," said the man, "do you have a few minutes for us to share a story with you?"

"Absolutely," I replied. "All my books are based on the stories of real people. I love to listen—and learn."

"WE'RE MILLIONAIRES BECAUSE OF THE HOMES WE BOUGHT"

Their names were John and Lucy Martin. They looked to be in their early sixties, but young for their ages—fit and athletic—and excited about life.

"I hope you won't take this wrong," John began, "but we didn't actually come to the bookstore to hear you speak. We were just browsing when we heard the commotion in the back and thought we'd check it out. You were really engaging, so we decided to stay and listen."

"You were right with the advice you gave that young woman Karen," Lucy piped in. "A house *is* the best investment you'll ever make."

"And renting never makes sense if you can avoid it," John added.

John and Lucy looked at each other and smiled. "We know from personal experience," said John. "In fact, we're millionaires today because of the homes we bought over the years."

"Really?" I said.

"Now don't misunderstand," John continued. "I don't mean to boast. It's just that I think it's really frightening how many of these young kids seem to be making so much money in the stock market so quickly. They don't realize that all those dot-com profits are just on paper—and that until they sell their stock and invest in something like a home, it's nothing but pure speculation." This was the 1990s, and John was wise to be skeptical.

"WHAT MADE US RICH WAS HOMEOWNERSHIP"

Lucy nodded vigorously. "We've invested in the stock market ourselves over the years, but we've always been well-diversified and in it for the long haul," she said.

I nodded in agreement.

"But here's the thing," Lucy went on, "what made us rich was being homeowners. When we were young, we never thought we'd be able to even buy a home. But it turned out to be so much easier than we imagined—and ultimately it helped us build real financial security."

John beamed proudly. "I still find it hard to believe, but we own more than $3 million worth of real estate. And we've done it simply by buying a handful of homes, living in them, and being smart about which ones we kept as rentals and which ones we sold for a tax-free profit. To tell the truth, it's been fun."

"And so much easier than we imagined," added Lucy. "Can we tell you how we did it? We'll take you out for a latte!"

We all laughed. In the presentation the Martins had just sat through, I'd been talking about what I call The Latte Factor®, a concept of mine that explains how the small things we spend money on (like lattes) can end up costing us a fortune—or make you rich if you learn to cut them out and pay yourself first.

So we headed off to a coffee shop—and a lesson about how to get rich through homeownership.

GETTING ON THE HOMEBUYING TRACK

John did most of the talking, but the story he told was definitely a joint effort. If anything, Lucy seemed to be the one who had originally gotten them on the homebuying track.

"We actually didn't buy our first home until we were in our late twenties," John started off. "And truth be told, we didn't really give much thought to money. I was in the military at the time and wasn't making much. But we weren't spending a lot either, because we lived on a military base and a lot of our living costs were covered. One thing that definitely helped was that the military had a bill-paying system where you could elect to have money taken out of your paycheque automatically. Basically, we saved money *automatically*, just the way you preached in your talk. We had a car we were paying for, so I had them take out the money for that. Then one day it was paid off, and we started discussing what to do with the extra cash that had been going to our car payments.

"It was Lucy's idea that we start saving for a house. My response was, 'Why should we save for a house when we can live on the base for practically nothing?' But Lucy insisted. She said that owning our own house would give us options. Renting would keep us trapped.

"Thank goodness I listened to her. Within two years, we had saved enough for a down payment."

"Don't make it sound so simple," Lucy interrupted with a smile. "Even then you weren't sure, were you, honey?"

John grinned back. "No, I wasn't," he admitted. "Our car was getting old and I was in the mood for a new one. But Lucy put her foot down. She said, 'No way. We're not wasting this money on a new car. We're going to go look for a house.'"

"That's right," Lucy agreed. "We were starting a family, and I told him we needed to move off the base and find us a nice neighbourhood with a good school system."

THE NEIGHBOURHOOD WASN'T IDEAL, BUT THE HOUSE WAS AFFORDABLE

John resumed the story. "At first, it seemed pretty impossible. As we began looking, we quickly realized that we couldn't afford very much. It was hard because we'd both grown up in nice homes. Our parents certainly weren't rich, but things were cheaper in their day. The homes we were being shown were insanely expensive.

"To make matters worse, our friends were giving us a hard time for wanting to leave the base, telling us we were wasting our time. But Lucy was relentless. Every Sunday, we pored through the paper to see what was out there. We went to open houses on weekends and drove around neighbourhoods we liked, looking for 'For Sale' signs. But the more we looked, the more depressed we became. It seemed like nothing was in our price range in the places where we wanted to live.

"We were about to give up when we saw an article in the paper about this area called Walnut Creek. Back then, Walnut Creek was in the middle of nowhere, in the absolute boondocks. But the houses were affordable and the schools were good, and more and more young couples were moving out there.

"We called a real estate agent in the area and went out looking with her. In two days, we found a home for $30,000. Now, Walnut Creek really wasn't where we wanted to live. It was about twenty minutes farther out than we wanted to be. And the house wasn't perfect. It was small and it needed a lot of sweat equity, as they say. But it had three bedrooms and two baths, and we felt we could afford it. We had enough saved for a down payment, and we felt that with a lot of belt-tightening we could make the mortgage payments. Still, back then, $30,000 seemed like a fortune to us."

"YOU START SMALL AND
YOU WORK YOUR WAY UP"

"While we were looking at the house, Lucy noticed I wasn't too excited about it. I think I even said to her, 'You know, this isn't exactly the dream house we've always talked about.' And she said, 'John, dreams start small.' And then our real estate agent said something I've never forgotten. She said, 'You don't buy your dream house with your first purchase, but it will be your first house that someday helps you get your dream house.'

"We realized she was right, and then and there Lucy and I made the decision to go for it. We made an offer and it got accepted."

A $30,000 INVESTMENT EVENTUALLY
TURNS INTO $1 MILLION

John leaned back in his chair, a faraway look in his eye as he recalled that fateful day. "That was nearly thirty-five years ago," he said. "Today, that little house is worth nearly a million dollars. I know because we still own it."

"We paid off the mortgage years ago," Lucy chimed in, "and we rent it now to a nice young couple with kids. They pay us nearly $3,000 a month. Hard to believe we bought it for less than it now brings us in rent in a single year."

"Our second house was a lot more expensive," John said,

resuming the story. "It cost us a little over $100,000. Of course, it was bigger and it was in a new development—with a pool!"

"We needed both the space and the pool," Lucy laughed. "By then, we had three kids."

"And even though I was out of the service by then and making a little more money, we once again had to stretch to make the purchase," John continued. "But—and this is really important—we didn't stretch too much to buy it. In fact, we actually stretched a little *less* than we could afford because we had decided not to sell our first house but, instead, to keep it and rent it out. So instead of selling, we refinanced just enough to pull out a down payment on our new place."

SAVING A TON OF MONEY BY PAYING OFF THE MORTGAGE EARLY

"By the time our kids went off to university, our $100,000 house was worth more than $500,000. We truly couldn't believe it."

"And best of all," Lucy added, "it was nearly paid off because we had used a program our bank offered called a 'biweekly mortgage payment plan.' It sounds complicated but it's not. What it does is help you pay off your mortgage extra fast, which saves you tons of money in interest."

"You know the saying, 'Time is money'?" John interjected. "Well, with mortgages, that's really true."

"Which is why in addition to using the biweekly mortgage

payment plan, we also added a little extra to our mortgage payment at the end of the year when John got his bonus," said Lucy.

John nodded and gestured to Lucy. "Why don't you tell the rest of the story, hon?"

Lucy plunged ahead. "With our kids out of university, we really didn't need to worry about school systems anymore. John wanted to live on a golf course, and so we started looking around at golf communities."

"WE DID SOMETHING CRAZY— WE BOUGHT OUR DREAM HOUSE!"

"Long story short, we sold our second home for $650,000. And then we did something crazy with the money—we used it to buy our dream house! It was 4,000 square feet, with a pool. The price was $750,000, so once again we had to stretch a bit. But interest rates had come down a lot and we felt we could make the payments.

"We couldn't believe it. Little us, now living in a huge house, almost a mansion. It was nearly five times the size of our first house and three times the size of the houses we grew up in. Our kids thought we were crazy. But we were ready for some fun."

"Still are!" exclaimed John, and we all laughed.

"Well, that was ten years ago," Lucy went on. "We recently sold that house for more than $2 million. We spent part of the money on a new house on a golf course in Arizona, which is where we live now, and the rest to buy a small apartment building. The building has four units, and makes us about $50,000 a year in rent after expenses. Between our first house, which we rent out, and this four-plex, we earn $90,000 a year. Not bad for a retired couple."

LIVING IT UP WITH
NO FINANCIAL WORRIES

"And you know the most amazing thing about it all?" John asked. "We really didn't do anything all that special. But here we are 35 years later living it up, retired with no financial worries and a wonderful home on a golf course."

"Oh, come on," I said, "you're selling yourselves short. What you did really *was* special."

John shook his head. "Not at all. We always took care not to overextend ourselves. If we did anything at all special it was not to sell our first home. Renting out that house helped us build equity at someone else's expense. And ultimately, the rent from that house helped us pay down the mortgage on the house we were living in much faster."

"Because of that," said Lucy, "when we were ready to buy our third home, we were able to afford a really big one."

"We plan to do even better with the home we have now," John said. "We're going to sell it as soon as its value increases by $500,000."

"EVEN IF OUR HOUSE DOESN'T APPRECIATE, WE'LL STILL BE FINE"

"You mean *if* its value goes up, John," added Lucy. "Even in real estate, nothing is guaranteed. Of course, if our house doesn't appreciate, we'll still be fine, living in it and enjoying ourselves."

John laughed appreciatively. "That's my Lucy. Always the realist. *If* it goes up by $500,000."

He patted Lucy on the arm. "It's really something," he said. "I suppose we've been luckier than a lot of people. We certainly aren't the smartest folks around. But all in all, it really hasn't taken much effort for us to do as well as we have. Sometimes real estate seems so simple. We don't even manage the four-plex we own. Our real estate agent set us up with a property-management company that does it for us."

"And don't forget that first home of ours," Lucy pointed out. "We've been renting it to the same family for ten years. Sometimes I feel bad for them. I mean, with all the rent they've paid us over the years, they could have bought their own home. But they seem happy. Not everyone wants to own a home, I guess."

"AND NOW OUR KIDS ARE DOING IT, TOO"

As we were heading out of the coffee shop, buzzed from our lattes, I asked John and Lucy one last question: "Do you think what you did over the last thirty-five years can still be done today?"

John and Lucy looked at each other and smiled. "David," Lucy said, "it's being done every day. Most of our friends are like us."

John nodded. "Our neighbourhood is filled with people who are doing what we just did. You know, even our kids are doing it. It's funny, our biggest mistake—mine and Lucy's—was that we didn't get started until we were practically in our thirties. Thank goodness, neither of our daughters waited that long. Veronica is only twenty-five and she already owns a condo that's doubled in three years. And her sister, Kathy, bought a home that's gone up by 50 percent. They learned from us how it easy it can be. Now they're teaching their friends how to do it—and they are already getting ready to buy second homes."

THE MOST IMPORTANT THING IS HAVING THE RIGHT MINDSET

"John is right," Lucy said, "but there is one thing he's leaving out. The most important thing about what we did was having the right mindset. *We were people who thought poor for a long time.* We thought we would always be tenants and for ten years we were. But then one day, we expanded our thinking. We realized that we could actually go from renting to owning. And then, when we got to the point where we were ready to buy a bigger house, we realized that instead of selling our first house, we could keep it and become land-lords. That changed everything."

She looked at me intently. **"Most people never change their mindset. If you do that, you can do what we did."**

I thought about what Lucy was saying. It sounded almost too easy to be true. "But what about discipline?" I asked. "I mean, it's one thing to decide to do something, but it's something else entirely to stick to that decision. Where did you get the discipline to put away the savings you needed and keep up with all those mortgage payments?"

"THE TRICK IS TO MAKE EVERYTHING AUTOMATIC"

John and Lucy burst out laughing. "Gosh," Lucy said, "we're probably the least disciplined people we know."

"The trick," John said, "is to make everything automatic. With the help of our bank, we automated everything from our savings programs to our mortgage payments. We even have our tenants deposit their rent payments automatically."

Lucy nodded thoughtfully. "It really is amazingly simple," she said, "I never imagined retirement could be so easy—or so much fun."

And with that I shook hands with John and Lucy, thanking them for the latte—and their story. Such nice people, I thought as I watched them walk down the street holding hands, such a simple plan.

They were, I realized, Automatic Millionaire Homeowners. Maybe someday I'd be one, too.

NOW IT'S YOUR TURN

The story of the Martins and how they got rich without a lot of effort or experience in real estate can become your story.

To find out how, turn the page and continue reading. You're about to enter the world of homeownership and real estate investing, a world that is far easier to understand—and to conquer—than you ever imagined. You are only a few hours away from a totally new way of thinking about where you live and how you live. If you're currently a tenant, you will not want to continue doing that much longer, I promise you. And if you already own your home, you'll soon be thinking about buying another one—maybe several.

You are on your way to becoming an *Automatic Millionaire Homeowner*.

CHAPTER TWO

WHY SMART HOMEOWNERS FINISH RICH

Lucy Martin wasn't exaggerating when she said that the most important factor in becoming an Automatic Millionaire Homeowner is having the right mindset. Most people think becoming rich is a matter of luck or fate—that it's the kind of thing that happens to some people but never to them and that the best they can do is just plug along and try to keep their heads above water. Like Lucy said, they think poor.

But if there's any one lesson to learn from the Martins' story it's that anyone can become rich. And it's not nearly as hard as most people imagine. The fact is, there are simple strategies that don't require you to make a lot of money or to turn your life upside down in order to live and finish rich. And one of the simplest and most effective of all is becoming a homeowner.

So where do we begin?

Maybe not where you would think. You might think we should start by talking about how much home you can afford. That's where most books on real estate begin. But here's what I know from experience: It doesn't matter how much you can afford to spend on a home or a rental property if you don't have the confidence you need to buy one. Deciding to buy your first house (or your second when you haven't even paid off the first) can seem like a huge, scary thing to do—which may be why so many of us keep renting even though we know we probably shouldn't. Unfortunately, it's not always easy to find the confidence to overcome the fear.

This chapter is designed to give you that confidence. Once you have it, you'll be prepared to act. And it's actions—not good intentions—that change your life.

This chapter is only twenty pages long. You should be able to read it in less than twenty minutes. That's not very much time, but in it I'm going to share with you everything you need to know about real estate and why it's not too late for you to buy a home and get rich.

NOTHING BEATS HOMEOWNERSHIP AS A ROUTE TO RICHES

Of all the secrets to financial security I can share with you, nothing beats homeownership. Nothing. If you do it right—

and that's not hard to do over time—you will ultimately make more money on your home than on any other investment you make. And, as I said before, if you buy a handful of homes over the course of your lifetime and rent them to other people, you won't just be financially secure, you'll be rich—maybe really rich!

This is exactly what happened to the Martins. It's what happened to me. It can happen to you.

As approaches to wealth go, home owning is a rather boring one—but it works. And it allows you to sleep really well at night.

LISTEN TO THE SKEPTICS
BUT KNOW THE FACTS

As I write this, the real estate skeptics are out in full force. They've been saying for five years now that the real estate boom is really just a bubble that is about to go bust. And in all fairness, they can cite some worrisome trends. One is the enormous amount of speculation currently taking place in frothy markets like Toronto, Vancouver, and Ottawa, where increasing numbers of people are buying preconstruction condos not as residences but with the idea of flipping them for a quick profit.

Given the enormous run-up in home prices, it would be surprising if speculators hadn't come swarming into the housing market. Everyone wants to make money fast. But if that's your goal, you've come to the wrong place. What we're talking about here isn't short-term speculation but long-term commitment. **This is a book about how to make solid decisions in real estate that will make you rich over a lifetime.**

I'm not promoting a get-rich-quick scheme here. I'm talking about a simple, timeless approach to living and finishing rich by investing in real estate.

How can I be so confident about the real estate road to riches? Well, the fact is that, with the exception of two periods—1981–82 and 1990–92—Canadian housing prices have climbed steadily since the mid-1950s through the late 1990s and into the early years of the twenty-first century, at an average annual rate of about 1.5 percent, according to a study by researchers at the University of Sherbrooke in Quebec. Between 1993 and 2003, real estate values in Canada appreciated at an average rate of 4.8 percent a year. In some areas of the country, such as Toronto, housing prices have risen by as much as 9 percent a year over the last three years.

This may not sound as impressive as the 9.1 percent return on the TSE 300 over the last decade. (Nor is it as impressive as real estate values in the U.S., which returned an average of 10.5 percent over the period.) But as we'll see in a moment, there's a big difference between investing your own money in the stock market and investing someone else's money in your home, and the difference comes when you cash in your investment.

If you still have doubts about whether owning real estate makes sense, here's something to think about: Four factors that make homeownership a reliable road to wealth and four reasons real estate is a good long-term bet. Spend the next ten minutes reading them. Then read them again.

When you're finished, you should understand why you need to own real estate. And then we'll jump into how you can go about getting some.

WHY OWNING REAL ESTATE
CAN MAKE YOU RICH

HOMEOWNER FACTOR NO. 1:
OWNING IS CHEAPER THAN RENTING

People who say it's cheaper to rent than to own are simply wrong. Under certain circumstances in certain markets (where real estate values are overheated and rents are low), there may be some short-term advantages to renting. But over the long haul, renting simply is not a good deal (except for the landlord whose mortgage you are paying).

If you don't own your own home, you can easily wind up spending more than half a million dollars on rent during the course of a lifetime—probably a lot more. Let's do the math. Say your rent is $1,500 a month. Over thirty years, that would add up to a total of $540,000 in monthly payments! But that's only if your rent never goes up—and whose rent stays the same for thirty years? Even with rent control, you're bound to have cost-of-living increases. And if you ever have to move—well, forget about it!

COMPARING RENTING TO
HOMEOWNERSHIP—LOOK AT THE NUMBERS

Let's try to be at least a little realistic. Assume you're renting a house for $1,500 a month. Now let's say you stay put for thirty years, during which time the landlord increases the rent by 5 percent a year. Over those thirty years, you will hand over to the landlord a total of nearly $1.2 million in rent payments—and at the end, you'll have nothing to show for it except a bunch of cancelled cheques. To add insult to injury, you'll now be paying him $6,174 a month! How's that for depressing?

Now let's imagine that instead of continuing to rent, you've used the tools you'll learn in this book to buy the same home for $200,000. Initially, your costs as a homeowner, including mortgage payments, taxes, and maintenance, are likely to total around the same $1,500 a month that you would have paid in rent. But these costs won't balloon over the years the way rent would. That's because your regular mortgage payment, which represents the lion's share of your monthly outlay, is fixed for the term of the mortgage.

What will balloon over the years is the value of your house. Say it goes up by 4.8 percent a year, the national average between 1993 and 2003. After twenty-five years, you will own a home that's worth more than $645,000. In some cities, where prices have risen at an even higher rate, your house will be worth even more. How amazing is that?

HOMEOWNER FACTOR NO. 2:
HOMEOWNERS GET LEVERAGE

What makes rich people really rich is leverage. Leverage is what you get when you use what is called "OPM," which stands for "other people's money." Buying properties with OPM gives you huge financial advantages, allowing you to multiply your gains. It's what you will use to buy real estate—the "other person" in this case being your bank or mortgage lender.

Here's how it works. Let's say you find a home you can buy for $250,000. Assuming the house really is worth that much, you shouldn't have too much trouble finding a bank to lend you at least 75 percent—or $187,500—of the purchase price. (As you will see in Chapter Five, you may even be able to get a bank to lend you more. But for now let's be conservative.)

This leaves you with a $62,500 down payment to make. You put up the cash, get a loan, and the house is yours.

Now let's say the value of the house goes up by 10 percent. So now it's worth $275,000, or $25,000 more than you originally paid for it.

If you were to sell the house at this point for $275,000, what kind of return do you think you would have just made? If your answer is 10 percent, you're mistaken.

Remember, you put down only $62,500 in cash. The bank put up the rest. But the bank doesn't share in your profits from the sale. They belong to you. The only thing due the bank is the repayment of the $187,500 you borrowed.

So you take the $275,000 that you got for the house and

you repay the bank its $187,500. That leaves you with more than $87,500—or roughly $25,000 more than the $62,500 you originally put down. To put it another way, you made a $25,000 profit on a $62,500 investment—which amounts to a 40 percent return.

But, remember, we were being conservative. As I write this, in hot markets like Toronto, Vancouver, and Ottawa, where real estate values have, in some cases, jumped more than 30 percent in the last five years, homebuyers have literally leveraged themselves into fortunes.

HOW LEVERAGE WORKS		
Assumes $40,000 down payment on a $200,000 house whose value increases by 6 percent a year		
	Value of House	Total Appreciation	Return on $40,000 Down Payment
AT START	$200,000	0	—
YEAR 1	$212,000	$12,000	30 percent
YEAR 2	$224,720	$24,720	62 percent
YEAR 3	$238,204	$38,203	96 percent
YEAR 4	$252,496	$52,495	131 percent
YEAR 5	$267,645	$67,645	169 percent
YEAR 6	$283,704	$83,704	209 percent
YEAR 7	$300,726	$100,726	252 percent
YEAR 8	$318,770	$118,770	297 percent
YEAR 9	$337,896	$137,896	345 percent
YEAR 10	$358,170	$158,170	395 percent

A great example of this is my friend Rick and his wife, Molly. Five years ago, they bought a house for $200,000. At the time, the developer was offering a special loan program with a bank that required them to make a down payment of only 5 percent. So Rick and Molly put down $10,000. Actually, they didn't have $10,000 in cash. They received $5,000 from their parents and put $5,000 on their credit cards. Their friends told them they were crazy, and even I advised them against borrowing their down payment. Most banks won't approve a mortgage to someone who does this. But they went ahead anyway.

Not long ago, they sold their home. Are you ready for this? The sale price was $400,000!

After paying back their parents and their credit cards, they pocketed nearly $200,000. Given that their initial investment was only $10,000, this amounts to a return of 2,000 percent in just five years!

As much as I like stocks, bonds, and mutual funds, there is little chance any of them will produce anything close to this kind of return. And there is no chance that anyone will lend you or me 80 percent of the purchase price to buy a stock, bond, or mutual fund. The same is true for gold, diamonds, artwork, stamps, limited partnerships—or whatever supposedly sure-thing investment you can think of. Financial Institutions simply won't lend people that kind of money to make those kinds of investments. When it comes to real estate, however, it's a different story. And the reason is simple—most people who buy a home will do anything to keep it. In fact, in 2004, banks in Canada foreclosed on fewer than 0.4 percent of all mortgage loans they made.

As a result, it's a lot easier than you may think to buy a house with someone else's money—and then enjoy the benefits of the resulting leverage.

> ### HOMEOWNER FACTOR NO. 3:
> ### HOMEOWNERS CAN EARN
> ### TAX-FREE PROFITS

Another way to stay poor (or at least middle class) is to keep letting the government take part of the profits you make from your investments. Buy shares in Research in Motion at $75 and sell them at $150, and you've made a bunch of money, but not as much as you think. This kind of profit is called a capital gain, and as with virtually all income, Canada Revenue Agency (CRA) insists on taking its cut. For most people, this means as much as 35 percent of your profit will go to Ottawa. If you held the stock for more than twelve months, it's a long-term gain and you get taxed at a lower but still hefty rate (from 5 percent to 15 percent, depending on your tax bracket).

There is one asset, however, that you can sell at a profit without having to pay capital gains taxes to the government. You guessed it—it's your home.

Remember my friends Rick and Molly, who bought a condo for $200,000 and sold it five years later for $400,000? Well, they didn't have to pay one penny of their $200,000 profit to the government. That's right. Zero. Nada.

Here's why. Under current tax law, if you sell your principal residence (which the government defines as a place where you live for most of the year and which you've designated on a CRA form), you don't have to pay any capital gains taxes on the profit.

So like Rick and Molly, you can buy a home for $200,000 and sell it for $400,000 and earn $200,000 in tax-free income. Not only that, but you can then turn around and buy another home for $500,000, sell it later for $1 million, and pocket $500,000 in completely tax free gains. And you can keep doing this, buying and selling and pocketing the profits tax free, as many times as you like for as long as you want—or at least as long as the tax code stays the way it is.

DOWNSIZE TO THE RIGHT SIZE

A great way to take advantage of this terrific tax break is to do what's called "trading down." I like to think of this as "downsizing to the right size." Rick and Molly are following this strategy. They found a really nice house in a gated community outside Calgary. The price was $350,000, so they used $87,500 of their $200,000 tax-free profit to make the 25 percent down payment. They're going to use the remaining $112,500 to buy another home that they're going to rent out. Because the tax-free sale left them with so much cash to put down, the mortgages on this rental property should be very low—meaning they will be generating positive cash flow from the very start.

See how this can get to be fun?

HOMEOWNER FACTOR NO. 4:
HOMEOWNERS BECOME SAVERS

One of the most important features of homeownership—and the thing about it most responsible for making homeowners rich—is that owning a home turns you into a saver. Why is this important? It's simple. People who have money have it because they saved it. People who don't didn't.

Homeownership creates savers. Each time you make a mortgage payment, you're saving money. That's because with each payment you're reducing your loan balance a little—and that in turn is building you equity. The longer you own your home, the more equity you build, the more you save—and the richer you get.

WHY REAL ESTATE IS A
GOOD LONG-TERM BET

By now you should have a good idea of the phenomenal financial advantages you get from owning versus renting. But change can be scary, and so can taking on big commitments like borrowing hundreds of thousands of dollars to buy a home. Lots of otherwise sensible people talk themselves out of becoming homeowners by convincing themselves that it's just too risky. But is that really true?

As I said earlier, this book is not about hype. So it's important to keep in mind that no investment—not stocks, not bonds, and not real estate—goes up in a straight line forever.

Like most other asset values, real estate prices are cyclical. They go up and they go down. And when they go down, they can stay down for a long time. In the early 1990s, real estate prices tumbled and then stayed flat for most of the decade. But in Canada over the long term (which is to say, ten years or more), there are many reasons experts believe that homeownership is an exceptionally smart way to invest your money.

Here are the top four:

> ### LONG-TERM REASON NO. 1:
> ### DEMOGRAPHIC CHANGE IS DRIVING
> ### DEMAND FOR HOUSING

Say the word "demographics" and most people's eyes glaze over. But for homeowners, demographics couldn't be more thrilling. The fact is that demographic trends—including high immigration, the aging of the babyboom generation and an increase in the number of single echo boomers—are combining in a way that guarantees demand for housing will stay strong for the foreseeable future, especially in B.C., Alberta, and Ontario. And continuing strong demand means prices are bound to keep rising.

Let's look at these trends individually.

• RECENT IMMIGRANTS ARE BUYING MORE HOMES THAN EVER BEFORE

Once they've gotten a job and started sending money to their relatives back home, one of the first things immigrants do when they come to Canada is start saving to buy a home. Why? Because owning a home is a key part of the Canadian experience—even for people who aren't yet Canadians. "For more than a decade," says a report from Statistics Canada, "immigration from abroad has been sustaining the size of our population and the formation of new households."

In 2001, says StatCan, over 40 percent of households that had arrived over the previous five years lived in a home owned by a family member.

Likewise, migration within Canada affects the demand for housing. People moving to a new area within the country need housing. True, they often leave a house behind, so their impact on the housing market evens out. But some people move from an expensive rental property in one town or city to another place where they can afford to buy a house. And this definitely keeps demand for housing strong.

• BABY BOOMERS ARE LIVING LONGER, AND YOUNG SINGLES ARE BUYING HOUSES

The baby boom of the 1950s and early 1960s has also played a major role in stoking the huge continuing demand for housing. As the nation's baby boomers reach retirement age over the next decade or so, they will continue to influence real estate markets.

For one thing, Canadians may be aging but they're also living longer and remaining in their homes as they get older. At the same time, more young Canadians than ever are living on their own in single-person households.

In fact, an increasing number of home buyers are single, divorced, or separated. In other words, instead of buying one house for two or more people, these individuals bought one house each.

Along with the falling birth rate, this has contributed to the long-term decline in average household size, from 3.9 in 1961 to 2.6 by 2001. This means that Canadians of all ages are buying more houses.

The amount of equity that baby boomers have in homes right now is staggering. According to the most recent comprehensive survey of wealth in Canada, conducted in 1999, equity in the principal residence accounted for about 36 percent of the average net worth of homeowners. The 54 percent of owners with mortgages had a median net worth of $113,000; owners without mortgages had a median net worth of $259,311. (We'll talk about the benefits of paying off your mortgage in a moment.)

The point is that, with home equity lines that banks are now providing, an increasing number of homeowners are turning their equity into hard dollars that they're using to buy second and third get away and vacation homes.

As a result, demand for housing has been strong. And it's expected to continue this way, particularly near major urban centres, around resort communities, and in "second home" markets generally. This is yet another reason to be bullish about the long-term prospects for real estate values.

• THE ECHO GENERATION

About one in ten Canadians, or three million people, are between the ages of eighteen and twenty-four. These Canadians are in the vanguard of the large baby boom echo generation, born in the 1980s and early 1990s. As they enter their twenties, they're raising the demand for housing.

Three main factors are helping to produce this "echo" effect in real estate markets: record low interest rates, parents willing to help with down payments, and inheritances.

This last factor is especially significant. Between now and 2020, the passing of the baby boom generation, not just in Canada but throughout North America, is expected to lead to the largest intergenerational transfer of wealth the world has ever seen. This record-setting inheritance boom is going to make it possible for more young people to buy more homes than any generation before them.

> ## LONG-TERM REASON NO. 2:
> ## IT'S EASIER TO GET FINANCING

The second reason real estate is such a good long-term bet has to do with changes in the way banks handle financing. It used to be that homebuyers didn't have many choices when it came to financing. You could get a twenty-five-year closed mortgage or you could get a fifteen-year closed mortgage. But then came the "creative financing" revolution. As a result, homebuyers today have literally dozens of mortgage options to select from.

These days, you can choose between open, convertible, and closed mortgages at fixed or variable rates, with or without rate caps, and with terms ranging from one year to twenty-five years. These options have emerged in an era of low interest rates, and it is likely that they're here to stay.

The vast array of available mortgages is a real boon to first-time homebuyers and experienced real estate investors alike, and there is no doubt that the proliferation of choices—and the increasingly easy access to it all—should keep the real estate market humming for years to come.

LONG-TERM REASON NO. 3: BANKS NOW LEND TO RISKIER BORROWERS

This reason is really important because it means that even if you have a bad credit record or owe a lot on your credit cards, you can still buy a home. To put it simply, the banking industry is increasingly willing to work with what are known as "sub-prime" borrowers—people who are self-employed, have had credit problems, or simply have a hard time proving they are creditworthy. That helps to explain why almost 90 percent of first-time home buyers between the ages of twenty-five and thirty-four have a mortgage. (In 1951, by comparison, only one-third of Canadian homeowners had a mortgage.)

My friends Jim and Rebecca are a great example of this trend. Over dinner one night, just before Rebecca gave birth to their first child, they mentioned they were looking for a two-bedroom rental to replace the one-bedroom apartment they had been renting for the previous seven years. "Guys, I have a better idea," I said. "You should be buying a place. Continuing to rent is just crazy."

A little embarrassed, Jim confessed that there was a house they had their eye on, but their credit really wasn't the best—and they owed about $25,000 in credit card debt.

"No one is going to lend us a dime with our credit," moaned Rebecca.

I replied that you won't know until you ask.

Sure enough, the first lender they contacted turned them down, as did the second and the third. But they kept trying, and after three more rejections they found a bank that was willing to give them the $250,000 mortgage that they needed. Because their credit was bad, the interest rate was high—around 9 percent—but they got high-ratio financing, which meant they needed a down payment of only 10 percent of the price of the house. The mortgage even covered their closing and some minor fix-up costs.

Three years later, they sold their home for more than $400,000. With the tax-free profits, they repaired their credit and paid off all their debts.

Increasing competition in the mortgage industry—and a growing realization among banks that lending to "sub-prime" borrowers like Jim and Rebecca isn't as risky as they used to think it was—means that more people who previously would have been shut out of the housing market will now be able to buy homes. The result will be more first-time homebuyers. And it's first-time homebuyers who ultimately drive the real estate market nationally.

LONG-TERM REASON NO. 4:
LOWER INTEREST RATES WILL LIKELY
EXTEND OVER THE LONG TERM

Canada's current housing boom was triggered by lower interest rates. According to StatCan, each percentage-point drop in interest rates between 1997 and 2003 inspired about 16,000 additional Canadians to buy their first home.

While no one can predict the future with absolute certainty, most long-term forecasts anticipate only a moderate increase in interest rates, which is good news for Canada's housing market.

NOW LET'S LOOK AT HOW
YOU CAN GET STARTED

If you still have any doubts about becoming a first-time homeowner or buying additional homes that you can rent out—go back and reread this chapter. Between the equity you can build, the appreciation you can expect, and the tax advantages you can enjoy when you sell, it should be clear to you that homeownership is as close to a financial no-brainer as you can get.

Congratulations on reading this far. Now, it's time to start talking strategy—to learn how to find the money you'll need to buy your home or investment property.

It's going to be easier than you ever thought possible.

AUTOMATIC MILLIONAIRE HOMEOWNER ACTION STEPS

From here on out, each chapter will end with a series of **Automatic Millionaire Action Steps**. These steps are meant to summarize what you just read and motivate you to take immediate powerful action. Remember, inspiration unused is merely entertainment. To become an Automatic Millionaire Homeowner, you need to act on what you've learned.

Reviewing the actions we laid out in this chapter, here's what you should be doing right now to become an Automatic Millionaire Homeowner. Check off each step as you accomplish it.

❏ Adopt the Automatic Millionaire Homeowner Mindset and recognize that anyone can become rich—even you.

❏ Understand the difference between short-term speculation and long-term commitment—and which one really will make you rich.

❏ Decide right now you want to be an Automatic Millionaire Homeowner.

CHAPTER THREE

THE AUTOMATIC DOWN PAYMENT SOLUTION

Now that you're ready to start building wealth through homeownership, it's time to talk "real world" about money—specifically, how much you're going to need to buy a house and where you're going to get it.

Given the steady run-up in prices over the years, it's easy to conclude that real estate has become a game for rich people only—that unless you've got piles of money lying around, you should forget about trying to play. In fact, nothing could be further from the truth. While having lots of hard cash in the bank can certainly make things easier, it's definitely not a necessity.

But before we get into the nitty-gritty of exactly how much—or, more accurately, how little—cash it takes to buy a home, there's an even bigger question we need to tackle.

HOW MUCH HOME CAN YOU AFFORD?

When it comes to investing in real estate, the bottom line isn't how much houses cost. It's how much you can afford to spend.

So how much home can you afford? There is no single answer to this important question—except maybe "more than you think."

And how much is that?

There are a number of ways to figure out how much you can afford to spend on a home. I think the most sensible rule of thumb is the one recommended by most banks and mortgage lenders. It says that most people can afford to spend about one-third of their gross income on housing (which is to say, mortgage payments, property taxes, and other regular costs). The following table should give you a good idea of the kind of price range your income would justify.

As the table on page 59 indicates, if you earn $50,000 a year, you should be able to afford to spend about $1,375 a month on housing, whether in the form of rent or mortgage payments. Different people will qualify for different amounts. Why? Because people earning the same income aren't necessarily in the same financial boat. Whether you should be on the high side or the low side of the banks' suggested range is a judgment call that each of us must make

WHAT PRICE RANGE IS RIGHT FOR YOU		
Annual Gross Income	Monthly Gross	One-third of Gross
$20,000	$1,667	$550
$30,000	$2,500	$825
$40,000	$3,333	$1,100
$50,000	$4,176	$1,375
$60,000	$5,000	$1,650
$70,000	$5,833	$1,925
$80,000	$6,667	$2,200
$90,000	$7,500	$2,475
$100,000	$8,333	$2,750

individually, since it depends on a number of factors. These include how much debt you are already carrying, what other financial goals or commitments you have (like retirement savings or special medical expenses), how secure your job is, and what your future prospects are. Obviously, if you have little or no debt, few other commitments, and are looking forward to a series of promotions at work, you can comfortably bump up higher than one-third of your income. If things are a little tight, you'll want to stay below it.

And while confidence and optimism are absolutely essential to success, don't get carried away. Keep in mind that most of us have a tendency to view our financial situation in overly rosy terms. Above all, remember Murphy's Law—the time-tested adage that says, "If something can go wrong, it will"— and knock 10 percent to 20 percent off whatever your calculations say you can afford.

Keeping in mind that home ownership (buying) is better than home loanership (renting), check out the next table. It shows what the monthly payments would be for different mortgage sizes amortized over twenty-five years with five-year terms, at different interest rates.

TYPICAL MORTGAGE PAYMENTS							
Monthly payments (principal and interest) for 25-year amortization with a 5-year term							
Mortgage Amount	5.0%	5.5%	6.0%	6.5%	7.0%	7.5%	8.0%
$100,000	$582	$610	$640	$670	$700	$732	$763
$150,000	$872	$916	$960	$1,005	$1,051	$1,097	$1,145
$200,000	$1,163	$1,221	$1,280	$1,340	$1,401	$1,463	$1,526
$250,000	$1,454	$1,526	$1,600	$1,675	$1,751	$1,829	$1,908
$300,000	$1,745	$1,831	$1,919	$2,009	$2,101	$2,195	$2,290
$350,000	$2,036	$2,136	$2,239	$2,344	$2,451	$2,560	$2,671
$400,000	$2,326	$2,442	$2,559	$2,679	$2,802	$2,926	$3,053
$450,000	$2,617	$2,747	$2,879	$3,014	$3,152	$3,292	$3,434
$500,000	$2,908	$3,052	$3,199	$3,349	$3,502	$3,658	$3,816

So what does this table tell us? Well, figuring an interest rate of around 6 percent (which, as I write this, is where five-year closed mortgages are), what the table says is that someone who can afford to spend between $1,200 and $1,700 a month on housing—that is, someone who earns $50,000 a year—could easily carry a $200,000 to $250,000 mortgage. In most parts of the country, that's still more than enough to buy a pretty substantial home.

YOU DON'T NEED A
BIG DOWN PAYMENT TO BUY

This is the most important truth there is about home buying. It costs a lot less than you think. And I'm not just talking about mortgage payments. I'm also talking about the number-one misconception that keeps people from buying a home or rental property—the mistaken idea that they won't be able to afford the down payment. In fact, studies show that this "no down payment" syndrome is the number-one factor that keeps people from looking at homes or believing they can ever buy one.

It used to be true that if you didn't have a lot saved for a down payment—say, at least 25 percent of the purchase price—you would find it hard to get a mortgage. But things have changed . . . radically. As I said earlier, you can buy a home with a down payment as small as just 5 percent of the purchase price, and sometimes a lender will even cover that amount. We'll get into the details of these programs in Chapter Five. Right now, all you need to know is that you don't have to be rich to buy a home. You just have to *want* to be rich.

That's not to say you can (or should) buy a home if you're totally broke. Even if you managed to get a mortgage that covers 100 percent of the purchase price (meaning you didn't have to make any down payment), you would still face what they call "closing costs"—fees for things like appraisals, inspections, title searches, and so on. These closing costs can easily run into the thousands of dollars. So you'll likely need to have some money in the bank. Before they'll give you a mortgage, most lenders will want to see bank or brokerage statements indicating that you've saved up a financial cushion hefty enough to cover at least three months' worth of such basic homeownership costs as mortgage payments, taxes, utilities, and insurance premiums. Usually lenders require their customer to have 1.5 percent of the purchase price for closing costs.

So even though you don't need to be rich to become a homeowner, you will need to have *some* money in the bank. With this in mind, let's look at how you can start immediately building up the funds you will need to get you on the road to becoming an *Automatic Millionaire Homeowner*.

SAVING FOR A HOME— AUTOMATICALLY

Remember John and Lucy Martin, my original Automatic Millionaire Homeowners? One of the things about their story that impressed me the most was how they used what had previously been their car payment money to fund what became their "home-buying account."

John Martin had his monthly car payment deducted from his paycheque. But once the car was paid off, the Martins didn't cancel the monthly deduction. Instead, they decided to redirect it to a credit union account they set up with the specific idea of saving for a home. It took them less than two years to reach their goal.

Setting up this home-buying account was their first step to homeownership—and to becoming Automatic Millionaire Homeowners. Now it's time for you to do the exact same thing. It's easy. Here's how.

OPEN YOUR "HOME SAVINGS ACCOUNT" AND GET STARTED

This doesn't need to be complicated. Today, as soon as you've finished reading this, make a date to go down to your local bank and open a savings account. Tell the bank you're not interested in an account that comes with an ATM card or chequing privileges (because you don't want to be tempted to spend any of the money you put into it). Rather, you're looking for an account that offers the highest interest rate available.

If you are starting with an initial deposit of less than $1,000, you may be quoted a very low interest rate. So shop around. Banks compete for customers like any other business.

NOW MAKE IT AUTOMATIC

There's no getting around it. In order for a savings plan to be effective, *the process has to be automatic.* Whatever you plan to do with the money you're saving—whether you intend to park it in a retirement account, stash it away as a security blanket, invest it in an education savings plan, or put it aside to help you buy a home—**you need to have a system that**

doesn't depend on you having to do anything. This means setting up a regular payroll deduction or chequing account transfer that automatically moves a specified amount of money to your savings account on a specific day of the month.

Having worked with clients as a financial advisor for many years, I can tell you that automatic plans are the only ones that really work. Clients would tell me all the time, "David, I'm super-disciplined. I'll put the money aside each month— I really will." They meant it. They believed it. But they were fooling themselves. Sticking to a savings plan is as hard as sticking to a diet—maybe harder. It's no accident that the Canadian savings rate dropped below zero in 2005. We live in a consumer society that's constantly urging us not to save but to spend and buy.

So why torture yourself? Make the process easy by making it automatic. This is exactly what the Martins did. Here's how you can do it.

> ## STEP ONE: ARRANGE FOR YOUR PAYCHEQUE TO BE DEPOSITED AUTOMATICALLY IN YOUR BANK ACCOUNT

The paycheque of most employed Canadians is deposited automatically into their bank account through their employers' direct-deposit service.

All you need to do is provide your employer with the number of your chequing account and the details about your bank and branch.

> ## STEP TWO: ARRANGE FOR AN AUTOMATIC FUNDS TRANSFER INTO YOUR HOME SAVINGS ACCOUNT

Since using direct deposit allows you to know exactly when your paycheque will be hitting your chequing account, you can now pick a specific day (or days) of the month for a specific amount of money to be automatically transferred from your chequing account to your Home Saving Account. If your paycheque gets deposited, say, on the 1st and 15th of each month, I would recommend that you have your bank make the transfer the very next business day (in this case, the 2nd and the 16th).

Most banks and financial institutions offer automatic funds transfer or systematic savings. President's Choice Financial, for example, calls its product the Interest First Savings Account. It can all be arranged in a matter of minutes with a simple phone call or visit to your bank's website.

MAKE IT EVEN EASIER BY DOING IT ONLINE

One way to make the process even easier—and to get some of the highest interest rates available—is to open your Home Savings Account online. As of this writing, Scotiabank is aggressively pursuing new customers with higher-interest-rate accounts that don't require you to maintain a minimum balance. (You can contact Scotiabank at **www.scotiabank.com**.)

As I write this in the fall of 2005, the rates on its high-yield savings account is 2.40 percent.

HOW MUCH SHOULD I SAVE?

Once you've got your Home Savings Account set up, how much should you transfer from your paycheque every two weeks? Obviously, that depends on your particular circumstances. But remember—saving up the money you'll need to become a homeowner should be your top financial priority. And that means digging deep and being serious about it— which, to my way of thinking, means putting away at least 15 percent of your pre-tax income.

SPEEDING UP THE PROCESS: FIVE SHORTCUTS TO HOMEOWNERSHIP

Even with automatic transfers, the process of saving enough money to cover even a small down payment *plus* closing costs *plus* a financial cushion can still take months or years. If that seems too long to wait, you might consider one of these five shortcuts to homeownership.

SHORTCUT NO. 1:
BORROW THE DOWN PAYMENT
FROM THE BANK

As I mentioned earlier, it is possible to buy a home without having to come up with the cash for a down payment. Some banks offer 100 percent mortgages, which cover the entire purchase price of a home. You'll still need to have some cash in the bank to cover the closing costs, but putting aside enough money for those costs and that three-month financial cushion won't take as long as saving up for a 5 percent to 25 percent down payment.

SHORTCUT NO. 2:
BORROW THE DOWN PAYMENT
FROM A RELATIVE

One result of the huge increase in real estate values is that there are more and more parents and grandparents who, because of the homeowners' equity they've built up over the years, are in a position to help their kids buy a home of their own. Don't misunderstand me: I'm not necessarily suggesting that this is something your parents or grandparents should do. (So, parents and grandparents, please don't blame me if you get asked!) As a rule, I discourage lending money to family members or getting involved in each other's financial affairs. That's because most such loans wind up becoming gifts. But there is an exception to every rule. I know from my experience as a financial advisor that, if there is one kind of family gift that makes sense, it's when parents give their kids the money they need to make a down payment on a home. The parents feel great about it, and the kids are grateful. And in many cases, the kids would have inherited the money anyway. They just get to put it to good use sooner.

All or part of the equity the client is putting into the purchase via down payment may be provided by way of a financial gift, as long as all of the following conditions are met:

1. The donor is an immediate relative of the borrower.
2. The lender has verified that the money is a genuine gift.
3. The lender has verified at least fifteen days prior to the closing date that the gift money has been transferred to the borrower.

The Lender, in most cases, will verify the authenticity of the gift by obtaining a written confirmation, signed by the donor and the borrower, which will confirm the following:

1. The money is a genuine gift from the donor and does not ever have to be repaid.
2. No part of the gift is being provided by any third party having any interest in the sale of the property.

SHORTCUT NO. 3:
BORROW THE DOWN PAYMENT
FROM YOUR RETIREMENT PLAN

Another potential source of funds for a down payment may be your retirement plan.

If you're a first-time homebuyer, you can borrow money from your own RRSP for a down payment—as much as $20,000—and take as long as fifteen years to pay it back.

Called the Home Buyers Plan, you qualify if you haven't owned a home in the past five years. Your partner can borrow the same amount, which gives you a combined maximum of $40,000 for a down payment.

The money doesn't count as part of your income for tax purposes. And you don't have to start repaying the money for as long as two years after you borrow it.

The Canada Mortgage and Housing Corporation (CMHC) website (**www.cmhc-schl.gc.ca**) describes this program in more detail.

A WARNING ABOUT BORROWING FROM YOUR RETIREMENT PLAN

The warning about this really being a loan is no minor detail. If you don't repay one-fifteenth of the loan every year for fifteen years, Ottawa will regard the loan as part of your income and tax you accordingly.

SHORTCUT NO. 4:
MAKE A RADICAL LIFE CHANGE

What keeps many tenants from buying a home—or homeowners from investing in a rental property—is that they're not willing to change their current lifestyle in order to get what they really want. Every day, I meet people who live in great apartments, lease great cars, and wear wonderful clothes. But they tell me they can't save for the home they want because they are living paycheque to paycheque!

My response is always the same: "Well, how about downsizing your lifestyle a little? Move into a smaller apartment. Live in a less fashionable neighbourhood. Drive a less expensive car. Buy fewer clothes. Eat out a little less. Make some changes."

More often than not, they'll shrug and say, "You're right— I *should* do that." And then a year later, I'll run into them and find they're still renting.

Fortunately, there are also exceptions to the rule, people who take charge of their lives and make things happen!

SIX MONTHS OF SACRIFICE— A LIFETIME OF FINANCIAL FREEDOM

My friend George is a great example of this. When he and his wife, Donna, first got married, they were renting an apartment in Vancouver. They really wanted to buy a home, but no matter how hard they tried, they couldn't seem to save enough.

After complaining for a while about the incredibly high price of housing in Vancouver, they did something life-changing. In order to be able to save what they needed for a down payment, they moved in with Donna's father for six months.

They'd just had their first child, and I remember George saying to me, "David, I don't know if we'll be able to make this work. I mean, Donna's dad is amazing, and we're really lucky that he offered to put us up. But can you imagine being married with a kid and living with your parents to save money?"

As it turned out, George and Donna survived living with Donna's dad just fine. In fact, it was great for everyone. Donna's dad got to spend time with his grandson—and

Donna and George were able to save every dime they earned for six months. They used the money to put a down payment on a little house in an area that was not yet booming. The place needed work, and it was about thirty minutes farther out than they wanted to live, but it cost them only $225,000.

That was six years ago. Today, the house is worth more than $500,000! Just last year, George and Donna refinanced the place and pulled some money out so that George could realize his longtime goal of running his own business. He and Donna are now living their dreams—all because they were willing to make just a six-month change in their lifestyle.

What kind of lifestyle change could you make right now to have the future you want?

SHORTCUT NO.5:
FIND YOUR LATTE FACTOR AND DOUBLE LATTE FACTOR®

There wasn't any way I could write this book and not slip this in. If you've read any of my other books, seen me on television, heard me on the radio, or come across my philosophies in a newspaper or magazine interview, you know the Latte Factor is my "mantra." It's my metaphor for how we all spend lots of money on little things—and how we can save ourselves a fortune (maybe a down payment) if we just start keeping track of where it goes and holding onto some of it.

This idea has changed so many people's lives that it's worth repeating. And if you haven't heard of the Latte Factor or Double Latte Factor, you need to. So here goes.

USING THE LATTE FACTOR TO FIND
THE MONEY FOR A DOWN PAYMENT

We've all got more money than we think. The problem is that we often waste it on small things that we want but don't really need.

The fastest way to save money for a home (or anything else, for that matter) is for you to figure out where all your hard-earned money is going—and then learn to hang on to it rather than spend it. This is the essence of the Latte Factor. For example, say you go to Starbucks every morning and get a grande nonfat latte. Right there, you're looking at about four bucks! Add a nonfat muffin to that and you've spent closer to $7!

Drop $7 a day on a latte and a nonfat muffin, and you're spending $210 a month on coffee and muffins. That's about $2,500 a year. Hmm—where else in your life are you wasting money like this? Maybe it's not on lattes. And don't get me wrong—I'm not picking on coffee. I happen to like a good latte from Starbucks every once in a while myself. *As I said, the Latte Factor is a metaphor.*

Could your weakness be bottled water? Bottled water is a $7 billion a year industry in North America. How much of that came out of your pocket this month? Maybe it's cigarettes. You can easily spend $300 a month on cigarettes. If you rent and you smoke—stop smoking! You'll be able to become a homeowner in only a few years, and you'll live longer. Seriously.

If you're looking for a fast way to save for a home, the bottom line is that it's all about the small stuff. Finding your Latte Factor can really help you see that you're already earning enough to be able to save for a home. Your problem is just that you're spending too much of it. Change your habits for twelve months, and before you know it, you'll have what you need to buy a home.

THE DOUBLE LATTE FACTOR—
THE FASTEST WAY TO FIND THE MONEY

The Double Latte Factor (a concept I introduced in my last book, *Start Late, Finish Rich*) is something you use when you really want to make the most of what you earn. The idea here is that you take a hard look at your fixed overhead (that is, your regular monthly costs) and then cut them back a little.

A great example is cable TV service. Let's say you've got a typical deluxe cable package and you're spending $80 a month on 200 channels, 190 of which you never watch. I'm not suggesting you give up your television. Just cut back to basic cable service and knock your monthly bill down to $29. That alone would save you an additional $600 a year that you could put toward a down payment on a house.

Then there's your phone bill. Do you really need both a regular home phone *and* a cell phone? If you let your home phone go, you could probably save another $500 a year! And that cell phone bill—do you really use 1,000 minutes a month? Couldn't you save another $30 a month by reducing the minutes and not going over each month? That could help you save another $400 a year.

The Latte Factor and the Double Latte Factor are designed to help you focus on precisely how you spend money.

Remember, the faster you can figure out where your money is going, the faster you will be able to save. And the faster you can save, the faster you will achieve your dream of becoming an Automatic Millionaire Homeowner.

So with this in mind, go find your Latte Factor! Use the form on the next page to figure out where your money is going—and then start channeling more of it into your Home Savings Account.

TAKE THE DOUBLE LATTE FACTOR CHALLENGE—AND WIN A FREE LATTE MUG

You can win a free Latte Factor mug (perfect for drinking your home-brewed coffee) by sharing your Latte or Double Latte Factor experience in an e-mail to me at success@ finishrich.com. Just tell me what happened to you when you took the challenge. How much money did you find? What did you learn? We'll select a new winner every day!

Since making similar offers in *The Automatic Millionaire* and *Start Late, Finish Rich,* I've received thousands of success stories from readers around the world. It's a simple idea that is really working. I urge you to visit my website at **www.finishrich.com** and read how the Latte Factor is changing the lives of people just like you. Maybe their stories will inspire you. Maybe your story will wind up inspiring someone else!

THE DOUBLE LATTE FACTOR CHALLENGE

Calculating your Double Latte Factor means looking not just at your daily expenses, but at your weekly, monthly, seasonal, and annual expenses to find items and services big and small that can be eliminated or reduced for big savings.

Name: _____   Day: _____   Date: _____

	Item or Service	Cost	Wasted Money?		Amount Saved	Amount Saved Monthly
	What I bought or buy	How much I spent or spend	✓ If this can be eliminated	✓ If this can be reduced	I can save X amount by doing Y!	
Item Example	Bagel with cream cheese and small coffee	$3.50		✓	$2 per day by eating at home	$60
Service Example	Two cell phones for myself and Michelle	$200/mo including all extra fees		✓	$50/mo by changing service plans	$50
1						
2						
3						
4						
5						
6						
7						
8						
9						
10						
11						
12						
13						
14						
15						
My Double Latte Factor (Total Amount I Can Save Monthly)						$

HOW DO I KNOW WHEN I'M DONE?

Once you've found your Latte Factor and your Double Latte Factor, and you've programmed your automatic deposits to transfer as much as you can every time you get paid—and once you've added in your bonuses, birthday cheques, garage-sale proceeds, tax refunds, and office-pool winnings (you name it)—how do you know when you've saved enough? My advice is to save for a year or two and then buy as much house as you can afford with the down payment and cushion that you have amassed. Many people make the mistake of waiting for years to save enough to make a down payment on their "dream house"—with the result that they never get into a home at all. Remember what the Martins said—buying your dream home begins with the purchase of your first home.

Remember, your time in the market is money—so don't waste time and don't waste money. Go shopping for your home sooner rather than later.

NOW THE FUN BEGINS—LET'S GO FIND YOU A MORTGAGE

You now know how to save automatically for a down payment and closing costs on the purchase of a home. You've looked at some short cuts to the savings game, and you're working on finding extra money with the Latte Factor.

Now it's time to learn about the billions of dollars that are out there waiting for you to borrow so you can buy a home or rental property. The mortgage market is currently as exciting as it is confusing. But what really matters is that the huge number of financing options available these days makes home buying easier than ever before.

So let's find out where and how you can get the money it will take to make that home-buying dream of yours real.

AUTOMATIC MILLIONAIRE HOMEOWNER ACTION STEPS

Reviewing the actions we laid out in this chapter, here's what you should be doing right now to start saving for a down payment—automatically.

- ❏ Using the tables on pages 59 and 60, and adjusting for your particular circumstances, figure out what price house you should be considering.

- ❏ Arrange to have your paycheque automatically deposited directly into your bank account.

- ❏ Open a Home Savings Account and arrange to fund it with an automatic transfer from your regular bank account.

- ❏ Speed up the savings process by finding your Latte Factor and using the other shortcuts to homeownership.

- ❏ Visit **www.finishrich.com** and read the Latte Factor Success stories—then run your own numbers at the Latte Factor calculator in the resource area of the website. (And if you have a success story, share it with us!)

CHAPTER FOUR

HOW TO FIND A MORTGAGE ADVISOR YOU CAN TRUST

For most of us, buying a home is the biggest financial decision we'll ever make. Even if it's not the first time you've done it—even if you've bought two, three, or more homes in your lifetime—it's still a huge, huge step. And big steps can be scary.

So how do you get over the fear? Well, one way is to educate yourself so you can be sure of doing the right thing. *This is what you're doing right now.* The fact is that what you are learning in this book will make you smarter about buying a home and getting a mortgage than 95 percent of the people out there. And you can build on what you learn here by getting yourself some expert advice from a professional who can help you evaluate the many options available to you.

Everybody's circumstances are different. I can be your coach and guide, offering you encouragement and explaining to you the ins and outs of what can often be a complicated and confusing landscape. But without knowing the details of your situation, I can't tell you that one particular kind of mortgage product makes more sense for you than another. A good mortgage advisor, who knows *you and your finances*, can.

In this chapter, I'll show you first how to find one—and then how to work with him or her to make sure you get the best deal you can on a mortgage.

MORTGAGE ADVISORS— WHO THEY ARE AND WHAT THEY DO

There are two basic types of mortgage advisors. The first type is what is known as a "direct lender." They often work at a bank or other lending institution. Being a direct lender means that they are authorized to provide funds directly to the customer.

The second type of mortgage advisor is a mortgage broker. Mortgage brokers don't actually lend money themselves. Instead, they put you together with banks and other institutions that do, and they work with you to get your loan approved.

What direct lenders and brokers have in common is that both are sales people. Both earn their livings by putting mortgage customers (you) together with mortgage providers (the banks and other lending institutions that pay them). So they definitely have a financial incentive to sell you on something. The good ones, however, know that no one benefits when a consumer is persuaded to take a mortgage that's not right for him or her. The question, then, is how to find a good one.

DIRECT LENDERS VS. MORTGAGE BROKERS

The next time you're in your local bank, mention to one of the tellers that you're interested in a home mortgage. In most cases you'll be escorted to a desk in another part of the bank and introduced to a nice man or woman with a title like "investment advisor."

These people are typically trained to handle mortgage lending for the bank. Their job is to assist you in the process of applying for a mortgage. They will review your financial situation as well as your needs and goals and walk you through the process of obtaining a mortgage.

When you work with a mortgage banker, you are working with a direct lender. There are a number of advantages to doing this. For one thing, if the lender happens to be a bank and you already have an account with that bank, the advisor may offer you a "good customer" discount on your mortgage rate that could save you thousands of dollars in interest over the life of your loan. Also banks service their own loans (that is, handle the monthly billing) themselves, rather than outsourcing it to some company you've never heard of. They do this because they want to make sure that you're well taken care of, so you'll come back to them the next time you need a loan.

Working with a direct lender can also be an advantage when it's time to renew and refinance. (Renewing means signing up for another mortgage when the term of your current mortgage ends. Refinancing means paying off your first mortgage and taking out a new mortgage.) Because your bank is already familiar with you and your house, you can often renew in minutes. I once refinanced my home with my bank while lying by a pool in Hawaii. The whole process took ten minutes, and saved me thousands of dollars.

Finally, if you are looking to buy your first home, it may help to work with a direct lender because most specialize in helping first-time homebuyers, and they may offer special programs that can make it easier for you to get your mortgage.

Mortgage brokers, by contrast, don't work for a single bank. They are typically independent consultants, though they may work for a large national company. Unlike a mortgage banker, who represents his or her company, mortgage brokers don't represent any particular lender. So in addition to reviewing your financial situation, they will look at mortgage products from more than one company. They often refer to this as "shopping" your loan for the best deal. The key difference between mortgage brokers and bankers is that they can shop your loan to various lenders.

Common sense would tell you that a mortgage broker who shops your loan request to many sources should be able to get you a better deal than a banker, who is tied to just one institution. However, this is not always the case. As I noted earlier, if you are a customer of a bank, you might be able to get a better deal there than where a mortgage broker would place you. This is because many banks offer discounts to regular customers. That said, banks also get a lot of business from mortgage brokers and, to keep the business coming, they offer special deals to them as well.

The main advantage to using a mortgage broker is often specialization. There are mortgage brokers who specialize in the luxury market or loans for self-employed people or a particular loan product that a mortgage banker might not be familiar with.

Mortgage brokers can sometimes find money in unconventional places like pension funds. They also may have access to private individuals who want to lend their money to home buyers. Remember, very few people default on their mortgage, so it's a safe investment.

In most cases, you don't even have to pay a mortgage broker to find you a conventional mortgage. That's because mortgage brokers usually get paid by the lender, not the borrower. If you don't qualify for a conventional mortgage, you'll likely have to pay the broker a fee of 1 percent to 2 percent of the mortgage.

FINDING A MORTGAGE ADVISOR
YOU CAN TRUST

Not all advisors are the same. You want to work with a really top-notch professional whom you can trust.

So how do you find one? The best financial people I know all give the same advice: ask for a recommendation from a friend in the business or someone you know who recently had a good experience getting a mortgage.

Well, that's fine if you know someone like that. But what if you don't?

Here's what I recommend. If you already bank with a bank, a trust company or a credit union, start there. Go into the branch where you usually conduct your banking and ask to meet with a mortgage specialist. Ask the person to review your situation, and see what the person can offer you. Ask if, based on your existing banking relationship, you qualify for any preferred rates. This may sound silly if you have a really small bank account, but you can never tell what you may be offered unless you ask! And the answer may be a resounding "Yes!"

Then, to make sure your bank is really doing the best it can for you, talk to a few mortgage companies. How do you find one? It's as simple as looking in your local paper in the real estate section. Read the ads: See who's offering what (including the banks and other lenders). Look at the advertisements and see whose pitch seems aimed at someone like you.

You can also find a mortgage advisor by checking the website of the Canadian Institute of Mortgage Brokers and Lenders, at **www.cimbl.ca**, or calling 1-888-442-4625.

Once you have identified an advisor who seems appropriate, call him or her and make an appointment to go in and discuss your situation.

Following is a list of questions to ask the mortgage advisors you meet with. I'd also ask these questions of an advisor who has been recommended by a friend.

It shouldn't take you much more than ten minutes to go through the list—and believe me, it will be worth the effort. Keep in mind that selecting a mortgage can be the biggest financial decision you ever make. Shaving just 1 percent off your interest rate on a $100,000 mortgage or reducing your amortization to fifteen years from twenty-five years will save you tens of thousands of dollars over the life of the loan! So take the time to choose the best advisor you can find.

FOUR QUESTIONS THAT WILL HELP YOU CHOOSE A GREAT MORTGAGE ADVISOR

QUESTION NO. 1: HOW LONG HAVE YOU BEEN IN THE BUSINESS?

It's important to know how much experience your mortgage advisor has. Selecting a mortgage is too important a decision for you to be willing to work with a rookie. (Sorry to those brand new in the business). Your mortgage advisor should have a minimum of three years experience and, ideally, more. In addition, ask candidates how many mortgages they arranged last year, and what type of mortgage products they tend to recommend and why. Make sure to ask if the mortgages they handled were for new purchases or refinancings. If you are looking to buy your first home and the advisor's experience is mainly with refinancings, he or she may not be the right one for you. A solid mortgage advisor should have arranged at least twenty-four purchase mortgages in the previous year; the higher the number, the better.

> ### QUESTION NO. 2:
> ### WHAT IS YOUR PROCESS FOR
> ### GETTING ME A MORTGAGE?

Applying for a mortgage is a lot like applying to university. There are all kinds of application forms to fill out, scores to worry about, and choices to make. Above all, it's important to make sure your expectations are in line with your abilities. Ask the mortgage advisor to spell out the process he or she will go through to help you do all these things. You should also ask the person whether he or she will help you get "pre-approved" for a mortgage and how long it is likely to take.

> ### QUESTION NO. 3:
> ### WHAT KIND OF MORTGAGES
> ### DO YOU RECOMMEND?

Good advisors will tell you they recommend mortgages based on the client's particular needs and situation. Of course, there are some who say this and then offer the same kind of mortgage to everyone. So ask which kinds of mortgages your potential advisors favour and why. If you're not comfortable with their explanations, or if you can't understand them, find someone else.

QUESTION NO. 4:
DO YOU SPECIALIZE IN A CERTAIN KIND OF CLIENT OR PRODUCT?

Some mortgage professionals welcome first-time homebuyers. Others work mainly with sophisticated investors. The key is to find a mortgage specialist who works with the type of borrower you happen to be. What's more, the size and type of loan he or she tends to do should be consistent with the kind of mortgage you're looking for. Obviously, if you have limited funds and intend to purchase a modest home, you don't want to hook up with an advisor who specializes in high-end clients looking to finance multi-million-dollar mansions. Similarly, if you're interested in a low-down-payment mortgage, you want a banker or broker with demonstrated know-how in this area.

IF YOU'RE NOT COMFORTABLE, KEEP ON LOOKING

The answers you get to these questions should give you a sense of whether the mortgage professional you're talking to is the right advisor for you. Chemistry should count for something, too. You're going to be discussing a lot of sensitive personal information with your mortgage advisor, so if you don't feel comfortable with him or her, the relationship is not going to work.

And don't settle for the lesser of two evils. If the professionals you meet with don't seem to be the right fit, thank them for their time and keep on looking.

IT'S TIME TO GO SHOPPING
FOR A MORTGAGE

It's amazing how far you've come. By now, you know how much you can afford to spend on a home. You know how much cash you have on hand for a down payment, closing costs, and a cushion. And you've found yourself a mortgage advisor who can help you through the process of actually getting a mortgage. So let's get going. You're ready to start shopping for financing.

AUTOMATIC MILLIONAIRE HOMEOWNER ACTION STEPS

Reviewing the actions we laid out in this chapter, here's what you should be doing right now to find yourself a mortgage advisor you can trust—and get yourself ready to start shopping for a home.

❏ See if you know anyone who can recommend a banker or mortgage broker they've worked with.

❏ Check the newspaper ads for a mortgage advisor who seems right for you and make an appointment to see him or her. Do the same at your bank.

❏ Based on your research and your meetings with at least one banker and one mortgage broker, select a mortgage advisor to work with.

CHAPTER FIVE

THE AUTOMATIC MILLIONAIRE HOMEOWNER RIGHT-FIT MORTGAGE PLAN

OK, so you're ready to buy a home.

Well, not quite. One of the most important things I can tell you about becoming an Automatic Millionaire Homeowner is before you start shopping for a home, you should shop for your mortgage.

You need to find the money first! After all, you may have all the confidence in the world that you can afford to carry a mortgage of a certain size, but if the bank isn't willing to lend you that much money, you're not going to get very far in the marketplace. And the truth is that until you meet with a mortgage professional and have him or her evaluate your situation, there's no way of knowing for sure how far the banks will be willing to go with you.

When you meet with a banker or mortgage broker—which is what you do when you go shopping for financing—you'll find out exactly how much you're going to be able to borrow and how much that borrowing is going to cost you. Knowing all this in advance is not only smart—it's the only sensible way to proceed. It will save you time, effort, and possibly heartache when you actually start looking at real estate. And most important, if you are worried about being caught in a real-estate bubble, the best thing you can do to "bubble-proof" your purchase is get the financing right.

Remember, it's not enough to be able to afford your home—*you ultimately have to be able to afford your mortgage!*

THE ABCs OF HOME FINANCING— WHAT IS A MORTGAGE?

The array of financing options available to homebuyers these days is truly vast. There are literally thousands of different kinds of mortgages to choose from. The question is, which one is the right fit for you? Don't worry if you have no idea how to answer that question. By the time you finish reading this chapter, you will.

So exactly what is a mortgage? Very simply, it's a loan you get—usually from a bank or other financial institution, but sometimes from the seller—so you can buy a house or other piece of real estate. What makes it a mortgage as opposed to an ordinary loan is that the collateral you put up to guarantee repayment happens to be the real estate you're using it to buy.

Let's say you decide to buy a home for $200,000, and let's say you've got enough money in the bank so you can pay 25 percent of the purchase price in cash ($50,000). That means you will need to borrow $150,000 to close the deal. This $150,000 loan will be your mortgage. You pay the seller $50,000 in cash, the lender gives him another $150,000, and you get legal title to the house—with one catch. If you fail to pay off the mortgage as promised, the lender can foreclose, evict you from the premises, and recover as much of its loan as it can by selling what used to be—but no longer is—your property.

Assuming you do make your payments on time, you will eventually build up what's called equity in your home. Your equity is basically the amount of your home's value that belongs to you. You calculate it by taking the house's fair market value and subtracting how much you owe on any mortgages you've taken out against it. Going back to the example I used above, if you've got a $150,000 mortgage on a house that's worth $200,000, you will have $50,000 in equity (which makes sense, since that's exactly the amount of the cash down payment you made). There are actually two ways to build equity—one is by paying off your mortgage, the other is when your home goes up in value.

THE 1-2-3-4s OF HOME FINANCING—
HOW A MORTGAGE WORKS

Mortgages have four basic components. There's the size of the mortgage (how much you're borrowing), the term of the mortgage (how much time you have before you have to renew it), the amortization (how much time in total that you have to pay off your mortgage) and the cost of the mortgage (how much interest the lender is charging you). Most mortgages have terms of one to five years, although you can now get a mortgage with a term of seven years or even longer. (The choice is yours). Many mortgages are amortized over twenty-five years, because the monthly (or biweekly) payments are more affordable than they would be with a shorter amortization. (If you have only fifteen years to pay off the mortgage, your payments will be larger.) The interest rate depends on the current state of the national economy as well as your financial condition, credit record and whether or not you plan to occupy the home you are buying. (We'll talk later about insured mortgages.)

When you're applying for a mortgage, your broker or banker may prepare a payment timetable—known as an amortization schedule—that shows how your monthly payments will be applied against your debt. With most mortgages, part of each payment will cover the interest charges you owe, while the rest will go to pay back what you actually borrowed—what bankers call the *principal*. Generally speaking, in the early years of a mortgage, the interest part of your monthly payment is much bigger than the principal part. As time goes by, and the amount of principal you still owe begins to decline, the proportion shifts: more of each payment goes to paying off the principal—until, at the very end, virtually everything is going to the principal and hardly anything to interest.

This is important to know because, as we will see in Chapter Nine, you can save big money by paying down your mortgage faster than the schedule calls for. (Most mortgage lenders allow you to make prepayments. But you should make sure of this before you sign up for a mortgage. Some lenders still charge a "prepayment penalty" if you want to pay off your mortgage early. As a rule, you should try to avoid mortgages that carry these kinds of penalties, though this may not always be possible.)

WHAT KINDS OF MORTGAGES ARE AVAILABLE—AND WHICH ONE IS BEST FOR YOU?

This is where the journey starts to get exhilarating—and maybe a little scary.

Shopping for a mortgage can be exhilarating because in recent years the mortgage-lending industry has come up with all sorts of creative products that make it easier for people not only to buy a home but also to buy more of a home because they can borrow more money.

It's sometimes scary for pretty much the same reason. There

are so many new mortgage products and styles of financing that it can make your head spin. And if you're not careful and pick the wrong type of mortgage, you can get hurt.

The good news here is that while there are more choices than ever, there are only a few factors that determine which is the right fit for you. Do you like taking risks or are you conservative? How long do you expect to own the house you're planning to buy? Is your income stream steady or erratic? Do you expect your income to grow significantly, or is your career mature? Do you have the cash for a down payment?

We'll start by looking at the most basic kinds of mortgages, then move to the more creative and exciting products—all with an eye toward which may be best for you.

Ready?

Great—let's go.

FIXED-RATE VS. FLOATING-RATE MORTGAGES

With a fixed rate, you pay interest at the same rate over the entire term of your mortgage, which can range from one to ten years. (At most financial institutions mortgages are available with fixed rate terms from six months to seven years. There are a few financial institutions that offer fixed rate terms of ten years—Royal Bank offers a twenty-five year term).

With a fixed-rate mortgage, you know that your interest rate won't change during the term you select. You can also increase your payments without affecting the interest rate you pay.

A floating-rate mortgage fluctuates according to the prevailing interest rate set by the Bank of Canada. Some floating-rate mortgages have floating payments that move with rate. Others have fixed payments. This means that while your monthly (or biweekly or semi-monthly) payment will likely stay the same, the amount of the payment that goes toward the principal will go up or down according to the interest rate at the time of the payment.

Floating-rate mortgages usually come with a lower interest rate than fixed-rate mortgages. At the time I'm writing this, in the fall of 2005, the rate for a five-year floating-rate mortgage is around 4.25 percent. The rate for a five-year fixed-rate mortgage is 6.1 percent. (Some people may get a discount off the posted rate based on their financial position.)

You pay less for a floating-rate mortgage because the lender isn't in danger of losing money if rates go up. You pay interest at the prevailing rate. With a fixed-rate mortgage, the lender could lose money if rates go up, because your interest rate stays the same for the length of the term.

When mortgage interest rates are low, locking in a rate for five or ten years can be really smart—particularly if you think you're going to be living in the home for more than five years. It's certainly the conservative way to go.

Fixed-rate mortgages are also attractive when you don't expect your income to go up very much in the future—say, because you've pretty much gone as far as you're going to go in your career or because either you or your spouse are planning to stop working.

Below is an important chart that shows where mortgage rates have been over the last twenty-five years. You can see they were lower between 2000 and 2005 than at any other time in that period.

As I write this in the fall of 2005, with rates on a 10-year closed mortgage running around 7 percent, I happen to think now is a GREAT time to lock in a long-term fixed rate. But who knows where rates will be when you read this? Look at the following table. It will give you some historical perspective on what to think about current rates. If they hit 7.5 percent for ten-year fixed mortgages, many people may tell you they are "too high" to lock in now. In fact, if you look at the table, you'll see that, historically, 7.5 percent is low. And if they do drop significantly sometime down the road (as they almost certainly will), you can always refinance. (Refinancing can sometimes cost you quite a bit in fees, but if you can get a much better interest rate, it can be worth it over the term of the loan.)

Historical Mortgage Rates
Annual Average Interest Rates

Source: PrimeRate.ca

VARIABLE-RATE MORTGAGES (VRMS)

With a VRM, you pay interest at the prevailing rate each month, although with some you make a fixed monthly payment over the term of the agreement. This means that the amount of principal and interest can change from one payment to the next if interest rates move up or down. If rates go up, you pay more interest and less principal. If rates go down, you pay more towards the principal and less towards the interest. In both cases, though, your payments remain the same. Other VRMs have payments that move with changes in rate.

A VRM is the most common type of floating-rate mortgage. VRMs allow lenders to adjust the interest rate to reflect fluctuations in the rates paid to depositors. When rates change drastically, as they did in the early 1980s, VRMs allowed lenders to raise or lower rates accordingly. Borrowers had to live with the possibility that interest rates would go up or down from one month to the next. In return, lenders permitted the borrower to convert the mortgage at any time.

You can pay off all or some of a variable-rate mortgage at any time, sometimes without penalty, or convert it to a fixed-rate mortgage.

CONVERTIBLE MORTGAGES

When interest rates are going up and down, you may want to consider a convertible mortgage.

With a convertible mortgage, you pay interest at a low fixed rate over a short term of six months or less. As with a variable-rate mortgage, you can convert at no cost to a longer, closed, fixed-term mortgage at any time.

With a convertible mortgage, your repayments are applied to principal and interest in equal proportions over the entire term, even if interest rates fluctuate.

OPEN VS. CLOSED MORTGAGES

A fully open mortgage allows you to pay off all or part of your loan at any time, without penalty. In return for this privilege, the lender will likely charge a slightly higher interest rate. But if you expect interest rates to fall, it may be worth your while. If you're right, you can refinance immediately at the lower rate.

During the 1980s and early 1990s, interest rates fluctuated drastically. As a result, most lenders stopped offering open mortgages, because they wanted to maintain some stability in their loan portfolios.

With interest rates more stable, however, lenders have started offering two- or three-year open mortgages. Many more offer open mortgages for short terms of six months to a year.

Some lenders offer partially open mortgages that allow you to repay a portion of the loan without penalty. Others negotiate a prepayment penalty in advance, so you'll know, for example, that you have to pay an additional three months' interest if you make an unscheduled payment against the principal.

"NO MONEY DOWN" MORTGAGE

If you're interested in buying a home sooner rather than later and you don't have a lot of money saved for a down payment, you should visit the local branch of a bank and ask them if they have a "no money down" loan program for first-time home-buyers. You may be pleasantly surprised to find that they do and that you qualify.

You'll still need enough money to cover the closing costs, although you can sometimes arrange a loan for this, as well.

UNDERSTAND THE RISKS OF
"NO DOWN PAYMENT" MORTGAGES

What can go wrong with borrowing the entire purchase price of a home? The answer is simple: If real estate values drop and you have no equity in your house, you can find yourself *owing more than your place is worth!* Should you be forced to sell your home under these circumstances, you wouldn't be able to get enough from the sale to cover what you owe the bank.

This is commonly referred to as being "upside down" in your real estate holdings. You'd be surprised how easily this can happen when things go wrong. So far in this book, I've given you examples of how the leverage you get from borrowing money to buy a home can make you rich in a rising market. Let me show how it can quickly make you poor in a falling one.

Say you buy a home for $300,000. The bank lends you the entire purchase price (all $300,000), so you don't have to put anything down. Everything is going great. You're comfortable making your mortgage payments. Your family loves the home. You're planning to live there for at least ten years. Life is wonderful.

Then one day you go to work and find out that your company has been acquired by a competitor. A week later you're let go.

No longer able to make your mortgage payments, you put your home up for sale. Unfortunately, the market has cooled. You try to sell the house for $300,000, which is what you paid for it (and what you owe the bank), but there are no takers. After three months, you lower the price to $275,000. It finally sells for $260,000. After paying the 6 percent commission to the real estate agents, you collect $244,400. That's $56,000 short of what you need to be able to pay back the bank. You don't have $56,000, so now what? This is when some people find themselves facing bankruptcy.

This scenario may seem unbelievably bad, but all it assumes is that real estate prices drop by 15 percent. In the last two years, real estate prices in Toronto went up by 9 percent a year! Think they can't go down 15 percent in six months? Think again.

I'm not telling you this to scare you off from buying a home with no money down. For many readers of this book, the ability to get a "no down payment" mortgage may be the difference between being able to buy a home now and having to continue to throw money away on rent for years to come.

I happen to believe that it's worth stretching yourself in order to get out of the rent rut. But you need to know the risks. And there are risks!

So if you plan to buy with no money down, consider your backup plan. If you suddenly lost your job and your income, would you be able to pay your mortgage until you got back on your feet again? Or might you be forced into a quick—and potentially disastrous—sale? Unless you have a secure safety net—like the possibility of a loan from your family or assets you could liquidate in an emergency or a payment plan you work out with your mortgage company—a "no money down" mortgage may be too risky for you.

PORTABILITY

If you buy a new home before the term of the mortgage expires on your current home, some lenders allow you take your mortgage with you. This is called portability.

Portability can save you money in several ways. First, you avoid a penalty for paying off your current mortgage prematurely, although you still have to pay legal fees to discharge the old mortgage and register the mortgage on the new property. Second, you avoid many of the costs involved in obtaining a new mortgage. And third, if interest rates have risen in the interim, you may be able to continue paying down your loan at the old rate. If you need a bigger mortgage, you'll pay what's called a "blended" rate—a combination of the old rate on your original mortgage and the current rate on the additional amount.

HIGH-RATIO INSURED MORTGAGE

If you can't scrape together 25 percent of the cost of the house or condominium that you want to buy, you might still qualify for a high-ratio mortgage, insured by the Canada Mortgage and Housing Corporation (CMHC), a crown corporation, or Genworth Financial Canada (Genworth Financial Canada is the new name for GE Capital), a private company. **With the help of one of these organizations, you can borrow as much as 95 percent of the purchase price.**

You arrange for the mortgage through the same channels such as a bank, a credit union or an insurance company, as you'd arrange a conventional mortgage.

For Canadians who can't put together a 25 percent down payment, Canada Mortgage and Housing Corporation or Genworth Financial Canada provides insurance for the lender so those Canadians can still buy a house.

To get a conventional uninsured mortgage, you need to have enough money to make a down payment of 25 percent or more of the value of a home. If you don't have that much money, you can pay a little extra and get an insured mortgage, so you can still buy the home. The extra costs could range as high as 2.9 percent of the mortgage. All these costs are incorporated into your mortgage payments, so you can pay them off over a period of years.

If this is the first home you've ever bought, you may qualify for a mortgage that covers as much as 95 percent of the cost and your bank will give you the 5 percent down payment. You also have to show that you can afford the payments and other costs of owning a home. CMHC and Genworth Financial Canada won't let you spend more than 32 percent of your gross income on home-related costs such as mortgage payments, property taxes, heat, and condo fees. And if you have credit card debt, a car loan, or other debts, CMHC and Genworth Financial Canada won't let you spend more than 40 percent of your income on these debts combined with your housing-related expenses. These limits apply to your total household income, including your partner's.

A NOTE ON RISK

Many of today's innovative mortgage products emerged in a time of skyrocketing home prices—an environment in which people could reasonably expect to "flip" properties so quickly that they would never have to worry about feeling the bite of a rising adjustable rate or finding themselves "upside down" in a falling market. This kind of party may be fun while it lasts, but it never lasts forever. Indeed, as I write this, the current one seems to be winding down. An Automatic Millionaire Homeowner is a long-term buyer who plans to live in his or her house for many years like the Martins did and weather the cycles of a real estate market that goes up AND down. This means getting yourself a mortgage that makes sense for the long term.

WHAT THE BANK IS WILLING TO LEND VS. WHAT YOU CAN AFFORD TO BORROW

Once you have shared your financial history with a lending institution, it will plug your data into a sophisticated computer program that crunches your numbers to come up with a mortgage amount and interest rate that the lender is willing to offer you.

Most mortgage lenders work hard to come up with a smart mortgage—one that will be profitable for them as well as manageable for you. But at the end of the day, if they get it wrong and let you borrow more than you can really handle, it's not just their problem. It's yours as well.

In the scramble for business, lenders have grown more willing to lend more money to more people with shakier credit. So keep in mind the guidelines I laid out in Chapter Three. The estimated cost of your monthly mortgage payment plus your other regular housing costs (like property taxes and insurance) should be around one-third of your gross income—exactly where depends on how robust your financial health happens to be.

And don't fool around with this. Do the math. Be realistic about your situation. Don't pretend you're in better shape than you really are. Look closely at the estimated mortgage costs and at how they compare to what the guidelines say you should be spending. If you're not sure how to go about figuring this out, there are plenty of online calculators that will help you crunch these numbers—including a "Homeowner Affordability Calculator" on my website at **www.finishrich.com** that will help you determine how much you can really afford.

CONGRATULATIONS—YOU ARE NOW OVER THE HARD PART

As I said at the beginning of this chapter, learning the basics of mortgage financing is often more difficult than actually finding a home to buy. Well, you've now done the heavy lifting. The hardest part is behind you. In the next chapter, we're going to look at how to get your best mortgage deal possible.

Keep going—you are doing great!

AUTOMATIC MILLIONAIRE HOMEOWNER ACTION STEPS

Reviewing the actions we laid out in this chapter, here's what you should be doing right now to determine which type of mortgage is the right fit for you.

❏ Understand that before you start shopping for a house, you need to shop for a mortgage.

❏ Based on the criteria laid out in this chapter, decide which type of mortgage product makes sense for you.

CHAPTER SIX

YOUR CREDIT SCORE: THE HOLY GRAIL OF MORTGAGE LENDING

Getting the best deal on a mortgage is not something that just happens. You've got to make it happen. But if you think that's something you can begin doing next week, you're in for a surprise. You've already begun the process of determining what kind of mortgage you are going to be able get. In fact, you started that process long before you ever even thought about trying to buy a home.

From the time you got your first credit card or took out your first student loan, you've been compiling what's known as a credit history. And it's your credit history, along with your income, assets and liabilities, that will govern whether you can get a great deal on a mortgage or one that's not so great.

In this chapter, we'll look at how lenders weigh your credit history—and then how you can make the most of it to get yourself the best possible deal on a mortgage.

UNDERSTANDING YOUR "FINANCIAL GPA"

It's funny how little time our schools spend teaching us about the simple things that really matter in the world. When you were in high school, did anyone ever bring up the subject of credit reports? Of course not. The only report that supposedly mattered was your school report card. Well, what about your financial test mark—your credit score? The fact is that when it comes time to borrow money for anything—whether it's a house, a car or your children's education—the first thing any lender will do is pull your credit report.

Your credit score is a number that the major credit-rating agencies calculate for you based on your credit history. Banks use this number to determine whether they will lend you money and, if so, what kind of interest rate they will charge.

For mortgage lenders—and borrowers—it's the Holy Grail. A high number means you've got a good credit history and, hence, are a good risk, so you'll likely qualify for loans at relatively low interest rates. A low number means you're a bad risk and will, as a result, probably have to pay a much higher interest rate—that is, if the bank is willing to lend you any money at all.

HOW YOUR CREDIT SCORE WORKS—
AND WHY IT MATTERS

The most influential credit-scoring system was developed back in 1989 by a company called Fair Isaac Corp. (FICO). The idea was to give lenders a quick and easy way to judge an individual's creditworthiness. What they call your FICO Score is a mathematical calculation based on twenty-two pieces of data about you that Fair Isaac gets from Equifax and TransUnion, the two main credit-reporting companies in Canada. Based on this calculation, you are rated on a scale that ranges from 350 (the lowest) to 900 (the highest). Anything over 700 is considered good. Score 750 or higher and the banks will give you their best deals. On the other hand, a score below 500 means you will have trouble getting a loan no matter how high an interest rate you're willing to pay.

If you qualify for a mortgage, your FICO score may affect the amount you pay for it. In fact, your credit score can make a difference of hundreds of dollars in mortgage interest payments each month—and tens, if not hundreds, of thousands of dollars over the life of the loan.

HOW TO FIND OUT YOUR
CREDIT REPORT—AND MORE

Knowing how you rate is essential knowledge for anyone even thinking of getting a mortgage.

You can get your credit report from one of Canada's two national credit bureaus.

Considering how much these reports will affect your ability to get the mortgage and loan rates you want, it's worth spending the time and money to check yours out.

You can get your credit report directly from Equifax and TransUnion. On written request they will each provide you with a free copy of your personal credit report (The credit bureaus in Canada are obligated by law to provide credit reports free of charge. They take their time about it, and you may not get yours for months after you apply.) For a charge of $15 to $22, you can also order a copy of your credit report online. Because they make money on these requests, the credit bureaus usually respond promptly.

Equifax Canada Inc.
www.equifax.ca
PO Box 190
Jean-Talon Station
Montreal, Quebec H1S 2Z2
800-465-7166

Trans Union of Canada
www.tuc.ca
Consumer Relations Centre
PO Box 338 L.C.D. 1
Hamilton, Ont. L8L 7W2
866-525-0262
In Quebec 877-713-3393

CHANCES ARE, THERE'S A MISTAKE IN YOUR REPORT

Having coached thousands of people on the process of both pulling and fixing their credit reports, I can tell you from experience that you will probably find some incorrect information in your credit report. Since these mistakes often make your credit history look worse than it really is, it's vitally important that you get them corrected as soon as possible.

It's actually not very difficult to do this. You can report any errors you find directly to the credit bureau whose report contained the mistake by going online to its website. At the same time, however, you should document your complaint by sending the credit bureau a letter via certified mail.

TO GET THE BEST DEAL ON YOUR MORTGAGE, YOU'VE GOT TO SHOP AROUND

Now that you understand what your credit report is—and what you can do to make sure it's accurate—it's time to go shopping for a mortgage. And when I say go shopping, I mean it.

When you go out to make a major purchase—say, a new car or a big appliance—you don't simply walk into the first showroom you see and accept the first price the salesperson quotes you. A good shopper goes to a number of different stores, compares offers, and even plays competing retailers against each other.

The same applies when you're shopping for a mortgage. Before you start considering offers, you need to have a good sense of what kinds of deals are available. And don't think that you can skip this part just because you've found yourself a mortgage advisor you can trust. Remember Ronald Reagan's advice about doing business when the stakes are high: "Trust, but verify."

What this means is that you need to do a little research.

DO SOME COMPARISON SHOPPING IN THE NEWSPAPERS AND ONLINE

These days it's easier than ever to find out what's happening in the mortgage markets. Just pick up your local newspaper. Most have a weekly real estate section that routinely includes tables listing what average rates are for different kinds of mortgages. The real estate section also tends to be chock full of advertisements from various lending institutions touting their best offers. So make a note of what's being advertised and where rates currently are.

After that, I would go online to do some investigative shopping. In a matter of minutes, you can become aware of different loan products and their pricing—and when it comes to getting a good deal, knowledge is power. My favorite mortgage-shopping websites are:

WEBSITES TO SHOP FOR A MORTGAGE

Banks: The websites of Canada's major banks are great sources of information about mortgages. In addition to answering all your questions, these sites provide calculators that tell you how much you can borrow, the different ways that you can structure your mortgage, and how much you'll have to earn to cover the payments. These tools are located at the banks' websites:

Bank of Montreal (**www.bmo.com**)
Scotiabank (**www.scotiabank.com**)
CIBC (**www.cibc.com**)
National Bank of Canada (**www.nbc.ca**)
Royal Bank (**www.royalbank.com**)
TD Canada Trust (**www.tdcanadatrust.com**)

Once you've checked out the website and calculated your mortgage eligibility, maximum affordable payment, and other variables, you can apply for a mortgage on the spot. It will take you about forty-five minutes to complete the application. You can then send it to the bank by e-mail or fax, and the bank will usually respond within two days. You can also take a hard copy of your application to the nearest bank branch and get an immediate response.

Canada Mortgage and Housing Corporation: Canada Mortgage and Housing Corporation website (**www.cmhc-schl.gc.ca**) goes into great detail about CMHC's products, including its mortgage loan insurance programs. (I'll deal with these in a moment.) You can also get lots of good information about what to look for when you go house hunting.

The Mortgage Centre: At a website called The Mortgage Centre (**www.mortgagecentre.com**), you can get competitive bids on your mortgage from more than twenty-five mortgage lenders, including banks like CIBC and Bank of Montreal, insurance companies like Equitable Life, and specialty lenders like Maple Trust and Xceed Mortgage Corporation. To get the deal done, you have to work with a mortgage specialist, who receives the lenders' bids and then advises you how to proceed. The Mortgage Centre's website lists the names and contact information of mortgage specialists in your area.

Online Mortgage Explorer Inc.: At Online Mortgage Explorer Inc. (**www.themortgage.com**), you can compare rates on mortgages of all shapes and sizes from a number of mortgage lenders including Bank of Montreal, Scotiabank, FirstLine Mortgages, HSBC Bank Canada, MCAP Mortgage Corporation, President's Choice Financial, and Sun Life Trust.

Royal LePage Ltd.: The real estate brokerage Royal LePage Ltd. (**www.royallepage.ca**) operates a mortgage service through its website that lets you apply for a pre-approved mortgage from President's Choice Financial.

In fact, mortgage-related websites seem to appear almost daily. You can locate more than seventy-five of them through Google (**www.google.ca**)

Spend an hour browsing these websites—both the ones that compare mortgages like **www.themortgage.com** and **www.mortgagecentre.com** and the ones run by national banks like **www.scotiabank.com**—and you will quickly get a sense of what kinds of deals are out there. In turn, this should give you some perspective on the deals your mortgage advisor may recommend to you. If the deals your advisor brings you don't seem as attractive as what you've seen in the newspapers or online, don't hesitate to ask why. In many cases, you may find that's because the rates quoted in the ads are for products that won't suit your needs. Or maybe you missed the fine print, and what you thought were really great deals in the newspapers or online aren't really so great after all. But don't assume that. Ask.

DON'T BE AFRAID TO ASK
FOR A BETTER DEAL

The simplest way to cut the cost of your mortgage is to ask for a better deal. You may not be able to get a better interest rate, but particularly when the loan is large, my experience is that a lender will often agree to give you a break on at least some of your closing costs.

Closing costs are the laundry list of miscellaneous fees, charges, and other last-minute catches that have to be paid before your mortgage really is a done deal. They are also a frustrating fly in the ointment that, if not handled right, can cost you dearly—and, not incidentally, take all the fun out of buying a house.

The fact is that closing costs vary widely—often by thousands of dollars—and many of them are negotiable. One of the most negotiable is appraisal fees. Here are some of the fees that you'll likely have to pay when you close on your home purchase.

APPRAISAL FEES

A lender can insist that your prospective home is first valued by a professional appraiser of the lender's choosing. But there are lower cost appraisal tools available to your lender that also confirm a home's value.

In some cases, the seller of a house may commission a professional appraiser to evaluate the property before putting it on the market.

SURVEY FEE

Lenders need a survey to confirm that the property you've used as collateral for your mortgage complies with all relevant bylaws, that new additions don't extend beyond the boundaries of the property, or that a neighbour won't dispute those boundaries.

In some cases, a lender will accept a survey provided by the seller, if it's up to date. In other cases, you'll have to arrange for the survey, either yourself or through your lawyer. Costs run from $400 to as much as $900. Some lenders will accept proof of title insurance, which you can buy for about $250, as an alternative to a survey.

MORTGAGE INSURANCE

If you obtain a high-ratio mortgage, you'll have to pay from 0.5 percent to 2.9 percent of the total amount for mortgage insurance provided by the Canada Mortgage and Housing Corporation or Genworth Financial Canada. This guarantees the lender that the loan will be repaid even if you default. The premium is usually added proportionately to your monthly mortgage payment, although you can pay it upfront if you have the money. There's no negotiating room here; the fee is established by a formula.

LAND TRANSFER TAX

Some provinces apply a tax to property transactions, called a land transfer tax. It's usually calculated as a percentage of the total cost of the property. In Ontario, for example, you'll pay one-half of one percent on the first $55,000, up to 2 percent of any amount over $400,000. If you live in Toronto an additional land transfer tax may apply.

PROVINCIAL FEES

Most provinces apply a fee for registering a mortgage and for transferring title of the property. These fees will usually appear on your lawyer's bill, and can amount to $100 or more.

LEGAL FEES

Lawyers charge a fee equivalent to about 1.25 percent of the price of an average house for preparing mortgage documents, searching the title of the property, and attending to all the legal details of transferring ownership of a house. They usually deduct their fees directly from the mortgage loan.

GOODS AND SERVICES TAX

You'll have to pay GST on your lawyer's services and on any other services involved in obtaining a mortgage. GST is also charged on new houses or condominiums but not on a resale property. If you pay less than $350,000 for the property, the GST is rebated. However, most new properties that fall into this category are sold net of GST. If not, you may be eligible for a rebate.

FIRE INSURANCE

Lenders require coverage of a mortgaged property against fire and damage. The policy must cover the replacement cost of the property. It must also give the lender of the first mortgage the rights to the proceeds if the property is destroyed by fire and has to be replaced.

The mortgage lender will require proof of insurance before advancing any funds. You should shop around for a policy. Some cost more than others.

TITLE INSURANCE

Several companies sell it, and some lenders will accept it in place of a survey.

GET AN ADVANCE COMMITMENT FROM A LENDER

Knowing that good mortgage deals are out there isn't enough. You want to be sure that one of them has your name on it—literally. This means getting a lender to give you an advance commitment for a particular mortgage at a particular rate before you even start looking for a house. With this kind of commitment in your pocket, you can begin your search secure in the knowledge that if and when you find a house you want to buy, you will be able to borrow the money you'll need on terms you can afford.

There are two types of commitments that lenders offer would-be homebuyers. One is called a "pre-qualification" and the other is called a "pre-approval." They may sound similar, but believe me—there's a huge difference between them.

"PRE-QUALIFIED" VS. "PRE-APPROVED" —THE CHOICE IS CLEAR

A "pre-qual" (as most professionals refer to it) is based on an informal review of your financial situation. The lender may ask you a series of basic financial questions (without requiring any written verification) and, based on your answers, give you an estimate of how much he or she thinks you'll be able to borrow. If you want, the lender will put this in writing, in what's generally known as a "pre-qual letter." You can then go out and look at real estate knowing that the lender "thinks" you should be able to get a loan for whatever amount is in the letter. The entire pre-qualification process can take as little as fifteen minutes. It's a snap.

Unfortunately, like most things that are so easy, it comes with a catch. The "pre-qual letter" is nothing more than a good-faith estimate by the lender—which is to say it's not binding. This means you can find a home, make an offer, have it accepted, and then hear from the lender, after he or she has completed a formal investigation of your credit record (which, among other things, will require you to document all the financial information you previously provided verbally),

"Oops, sorry, but now that we've seen all your financials, we can't provide you with the loan we thought we could."

This sort of thing happens all the time. That's why some experts say that pre-quals are not worth the paper they're printed on—and why most smart real estate agents these days insist that buyers get pre-approved for a mortgage, rather than just pre-qualified. Pre-approval carries weight because it means the lender has made a real commitment to loan you the money.

GETTING PRE-APPROVED FOR A MORTGAGE TAKES MORE TIME, BUT IT'S WORTH IT

Where pre-qualification is quick and informal, pre-approval involves a few more steps; pre-approval is binding provided all the information you give to your lender is accurate.

When you ask a lender to pre-approve you for a mortgage, you are asking him or her to formally review your financial situation, decide whether you are creditworthy, and then, assuming you are, commit to lending you a certain amount of money on particular terms, subject only to your finding an appropriate property and verification of your financial information.

To do all this, the lender will pull your credit report and score and study your credit history to see whether you can be trusted to pay your bills on time. The lender will probably want to verify both your current income and your employment history. He or she will want to see employment verification and copies of your tax returns for the last three years, especially if you are self-employed, and they will want to see a verified list of all your assets and liabilities. They may ask you for copies of your bank statements (often going back three to six months). In essence, the lender is looking for as clear and accurate a picture as possible of your financial situation. Can you afford the loan you want? Is it a safe bet that you would pay it back on time?

This review is quick, but verification may take several days to complete. But once it's done, you'll have a real commitment that you can literally bank on.

I strongly recommend that you take the time NOW—before you start looking at homes—to work with your mortgage advisor to get pre-approved by a lender. You're going to have to do this work eventually when you find a home you want to buy. So why put it off? It's so much smarter—and safer—to do it *before* you spend hours, days, or maybe months looking at real estate.

PUT ON YOUR WALKING SHOES— IT'S TIME TO START LOOKING AT HOUSES

Now that you've checked—and, if necessary, corrected—your credit report, found yourself a mortgage, and gotten yourself pre-approved, there's no reason to put it off any longer. You're fully prepared to go out and start shopping for a home!

In the next chapter, I'll guide you through my simple 10-step action plan to finding and buying a home.

AUTOMATIC MILLIONAIRE HOMEOWNER ACTION STEPS

Reviewing the actions we laid out in this chapter, here's what you should be doing right now to find yourself the best deal you can on a mortgage and get yourself pre-approved by a lender.

❑ Look in the newspapers and online to see what kind of mortgage deals are available.

❑ Get copies of your credit score and credit reports and arrange to correct any errors you find.

❑ Work with your mortgage advisor to get yourself pre-approved (NOT pre-qualified) for a mortgage.

❑ Negotiate your fees and closing costs to save yourself money.

CHAPTER SEVEN

FIND YOURSELF
A HOME
THE SMART WAY

You've got a budget and you've been pre-approved for a mortgage. Now you're ready to go out and start shopping for houses.

As I said before, one of the keys to becoming an *Automatic Millionaire Homeowner* is realizing that when you purchase a home, you are getting more than just a place to live. You are also making an investment that can become the foundation for your financial security.

Think about John and Lucy Martin. They weren't "super investors." They were—and are—normal people who earned a normal income, bought a few homes over the years, and used the equity they built up in those homes to leverage their way to real wealth.

You can do just what the Martins did. It may take you a decade or two . . . or three. But over time, you can buy homes, live well, and—if you act intelligently and deliberately— make some serious money. It's not always easy to do—but it is definitely doable.

Here's how to get started.

STEP ONE: MEET WITH A REAL ESTATE AGENT

One of the first things John and Lucy Martin did when they decided to look for a home was to call a real estate agent. They found their agent through the mortgage advisor they met at their local bank. You may be able to get a qualified referral from the advisor who helps you with your mortgage. A great real estate agent can make the entire process of home buying faster, easier, and more profitable. In fact, finding one is so important that I've dedicated an entire chapter to the subject. It follows this one. Read it carefully.

STEP TWO: IF YOU'RE RENTING A HOUSE OR CONDO, ASK YOUR LANDLORD IF HE'S INTERESTED IN SELLING

Here's something that very few people consider. If you're a tenant, and you happen to be renting a house or a condo that you really like, ask your landlord if he would consider selling it to you.

How likely is it that he will? Unless you ask—*you'll never know.* Maybe he needs the money. Maybe he's getting divorced. Maybe his kids are about to go to university or he wants to start his own business. Who knows? The only way you can find out is to ask!

The advantage of doing this is that you can negotiate a price without competition, your landlord doesn't have to pay a commission to a real estate agent (which could make him more willing to do a deal—and maybe even pass along some of his savings to you), and it won't cost you a penny to move.

STEP THREE: FIGURE OUT WHAT KIND OF PLACE YOU WANT TO LIVE IN

So you called your landlord and he or she won't sell. Or maybe you don't like where you currently live enough to want to buy it.

That's fine. It just means it's now time to go out and start looking at new places. The question is, what type of home do you want? Before you start looking, you need to figure out what you're looking for. Do you want a detached house with a nice little yard? Or would you rather live in a condo with a pool, a gym, and maybe a doorman? Are you a fixer-up type who likes hanging out in a hardware store, spending your weekends on do-it-yourself projects? Or would you rather buy a brand-new home in a brand-new development where everything is taken care of in advance right down to the carpets?

Before you go any further, you need to ask yourself some basic questions—and answer them as honestly as you can.

12 QUESTIONS YOU NEED TO ASK YOURSELF BEFORE YOU START LOOKING AT HOMES

1. Do I want a detached house, a townhouse, or a condo?
2. Am I willing to work on home-improvement projects after I buy?
3. Do I have the skills and motivation to make smart improvements?
4. Do I have the time and cash it will take to make improvements?
5. How many bedrooms and bathrooms do I want—and how many do I really need?
6. Do I want a garage?
7. Do I want a yard or pool?
8. Do I care about the school system?
9. Do I plan to be in the home for a long time, or will this be a short-term purchase?
10. Am I willing to commute—and, if so, how far?
11. Do I need to have convenient access to public transportation?
12. Am I looking at this home as a place to live or simply as an investment that I will sell or rent as quickly as possible?

At this point, it may be hard to be certain of all the answers. Just do your best with what you know now. Believe me, taking ten minutes to really consider these questions can wind up saving you a lot of time and frustration later on.

When I first got out of school, I bought a home with my best friend, Andrew, for $220,000. It was a three-bedroom, two-bath house in the suburbs that needed a lot of work. We were young, and we regarded the house as an investment. We figured we'd live in it for a year, then rent it out and move on to the next property.

As it turned out, what we thought would be only a few months of fix-up work ("just a little paint, some new floors and carpets") actually took us more than a year. Because we didn't have much money, we did most of it ourselves (including tiling the kitchen). That first year it seemed all we did after putting in seventy-hour weeks at our regular jobs was work on the house. For two guys in their early twenties, this wasn't exactly how we wanted to be spending our weekends.

In the end, the experience taught us a ton about buying real estate. For one thing, I learned that I was definitely not a fixer-upper kind of guy. I also found out I hated living in the suburbs.

The point is that you sometimes don't know what you like or don't like until after you buy. And that's okay. If life is about anything, it's about learning. All the same, you should do your best now to really think about these questions.

STEP FOUR: DECIDE WHERE YOU'RE GOING TO LOOK—AND THEN START LOOKING

You can't buy what you don't see. This means being disciplined and adjusting your expectations to match your means. Remember John and Lucy Martin's story. They wanted to be near the base, but the neighbourhoods nearby didn't have any houses in their price range. Still, they really wanted to become homeowners. So rather than doing what many people in their situation do—which is to give up and rationalize continuing to rent—they opened their minds to the possibility of living in a less expensive neighbourhood.

As a result, they began looking in an area that wasn't their ideal neighbourhood—at homes that weren't their dream homes. They weren't thrilled at having to lower their sights, but they were determined—and their discipline paid off for them in the long run.

SPEND YOUR WEEKEND GOING TO OPEN HOUSES

One of the most common techniques real estate agents use to sell a property is to hold an open house—that is, to open the place to the public for several hours (usually on a Saturday or Sunday) when anyone who is interested can drop by and check it out. You can usually find a listing of open houses—complete with times, addresses, and a short description of the property—in the weekend real estate section of your local newspaper.

So this weekend, check the open-house listings, make a list of the ones in your price range, then get in your car and go look at them. In a matter of hours, you'll be able to see as many as a dozen properties and get a real sense of what's out there that you can afford.

GET A MAP, DRAW A CIRCLE, AND CREATE YOUR TARGET MARKET

You don't have to travel all over the world to find yourself a home. Just draw a circle on a map that covers an area within an hour's drive from where you live. I promise you, somewhere within that circle you are going to find a home in your price range.

Now, like the Martins' first place, that home may not be ideally located. Their friends gave them a hard time about moving off the base, and the neighbourhood they could afford was twenty minutes further out than they wanted to be. But the schools were good, and if that's what it took for them to become a homeowner, then that's what they were going to do.

The bottom line is that you have to start somewhere.

IF YOU LIVE IN A CITY, TRY THE FIVE-MILE RULE

If you live in a city, you may not have to go so far afield. Just draw a five-mile circle around where you live. In an urban area, a circle that size will probably cover so much real estate that you'll be able to find a place you like and can afford within ten minutes of your current home.

Toronto is a classic example of this. Talk to virtually anyone under the age of thirty-five and, unless she's making a fortune, she'll tell you she can't afford to buy a home in Toronto. Of course she can't. The average price of a detached house in Toronto is currently more than $340,000! Even a condo costs almost $200,000. Can you believe that?

But downtown Toronto isn't the only place to live in the area. Get on the GO train and go just a few stops to the east or west (a trip that shouldn't take you much more than half an hour or so), and you'll find brand new homes starting at $200,000 in areas like Ajax or Mississauga. The smart people who took this train ride out of Toronto a few years ago and bought in these areas have made money, because their new neighbourhoods are now booming. Why? Because affordable neighbourhoods are in huge demand!

Even within a city, neighbourhoods that might seem down and out and crime ridden today can become desirable places to live. Such metamorphoses happen in cities throughout Canada. About fifty years ago, the Toronto neighbourhood of Rosedale was full of rooming houses. Rosedale is now predominantly a single-family community, and houses in Rosedale now cost more, on average, than houses in any other community in the country. There are other neighbourhoods in other cities that will inevitably go through the same transformation.

This is a really important point. Neighbourhoods that are farther out or older or even somewhat dangerous may not be "hot" right now, but this can change quickly as people like you who can't afford the trendy areas begin to move in.

STEP FIVE: USE THE INTERNET TO DO YOUR OWN RESEARCH

Because of the Internet, looking for real estate is easier than ever. These days, you can spend a couple of hours online and gather information about potential neighbourhoods that would have taken you months to assemble ten years ago.

The place where I'd start is Google (**www.google.com**), one of the most powerful search engines around. Just type in the name of the area you're interested in and add the words "real estate." Google will do the rest. You'll be amazed how much information you can accumulate without ever leaving your house.

Of course, while Google is a good place to start, it's not the only Internet resource you should use. There are countless real estate websites loaded with information about what's available, where, and for how much. Most of these are commercial sites run by the real estate firms and their agents, but, hey—you're looking to buy a house, and that's what they are selling.

MY FAVORITE REAL ESTATE WEBSITES

www.century21canada.com   www.coldwellbanker.ca

www.homes.com   www.mls.ca

www.realestate.ca   www.reals.ca

www.remax.ca   www.royallepage.ca

STEP SIX: CONSIDER BUYING IN NEW DEVELOPMENTS

As I write this, the market for new homes is absolutely booming. I can literally open a local newspaper in just about any community anywhere in the country and find a bunch of ads for new housing developments.

There are many exciting advantages to buying in one of these new developments. Here are six.

ADVANTAGE NO. 1:
NEW HAS WHAT THE MARKET DEMANDS

There really isn't anything like a new home or condo. Providing the builder did the job right, you get a brand new place with all the most popular amenities. Big or small, house or condo, if it's new, chances are it has been designed with an eye toward curb appeal. That's real estate jargon for the flashy features that potential buyers see from the curb and that make them want to whip out their chequebooks. These places also include features like bigger kitchens, more open space, larger closets, and bigger master baths.

This is important because, when it comes time to sell (especially if you plan to do so within five years), you want to be offering a property that other people will find desirable.

ADVANTAGE NO. 2: EVERYTHING WORKS

When you buy a new home, everything works—and if something doesn't, it's usually covered by a warranty that protects you for a least a year. Sure, you can always buy a homeowners policy to cover repairs in an older home, but your chances of having problems in an older property are much higher than in a new property, and even if your bills are covered, you don't need the hassle. Moreover, if the house is more than twenty years old, the problems—with plumbing, wiring, termites, foundations, etc.—can be endless. A new property isn't likely to have any of these woes.

ADVANTAGE NO. 3: DEVELOPERS CAN HELP YOU WITH FINANCING

In order to make the process of purchasing a home easier, major developers will help you with the financing—in some cases offering mortgages with down payments as small as just $1,000, in others offering deferred payments or low interest rates for a specified period, after which the rate adjusts. It's smart business for them, and it makes things easier for you.

ADVANTAGE NO. 4: NEW DEVELOPMENTS
ARE GENERALLY LOCATED
WHERE PEOPLE ARE MOVING TO

More often than not, the most important decision a builder makes when he plans a housing development is how much he is willing to pay for the land. A smart developer will tell you that if he makes a good deal on the land, he can pretty much guarantee his profits on the rest of the project. This usually means avoiding relatively expensive land in areas where people are living now and buying inexpensive land in areas that people will eventually be moving to.

How do developers identify these soon-to-be-hot areas? They spend millions studying demographic trends and analyzing population movements. They look at where new roads are being built, where new highways are being extended. Is there public transportation on the way? Is the city planning to build a new park in the area? Smart developers keep tabs on these sorts of things and buy up the land before regular people (like you and me) have a clue that anything is going on.

The point is that when you buy in a new development, especially if you buy from one of the bigger developers, you get the benefit of all the demographic research they've done to identify an area that's about to experience a boom. In other words, you often get in on the ground floor of what could be the next hot new area where homeowners are likely to enjoy major price appreciation.

ADVANTAGE NO. 5: NEW IS OFTEN
EASIER TO SELL THAN OLD

Sooner or later (and probably sooner), you will be selling your home. If you bought new, chances are your property will still be in good condition and, therefore, you won't have to spend a bunch of money to get it in shape to sell. What's more, if you're in a new development, there's likely to be built-in demand from potential buyers who missed out on the first phase and now really want to get in.

ADVANTAGE NO. 6: NEW IS OFTEN
EASIER TO RENT

In Chapter Ten, we will look at how to go from simply owning the home you live in to buying additional homes that you may rent out. For now, suffice it to say that if you are considering someday renting the home you are about to buy, you should be aware that it's usually a lot easier to rent a new home than a old one. What's more, you're bound to experience far fewer maintenance hassles.

STEP SEVEN:
CONSIDER BUYING A FIXER-UPPER

I just gave you five reasons why buying a new house can be a great investment. But that doesn't mean you should rule out buying an older one.

As I mentioned, my first experience with homebuying taught me I wasn't a fixer-up kind of guy. But that's me. Many people—including many of my clients and students—have made fortunes fixing up homes (and had a lot of fun at the same time).

The obvious advantage to buying a fixer-upper is that it's going to be less expensive than a house that's in great shape. Another advantage is that, after you've fixed it up, you may be able to turn around and sell it for a nice profit. This is how many people get started in real estate investing, and it's a great business for those who don't want to be landlords and deal with tenants.

One of my favourite examples of a successful fixer-upper comes from a former client of mine named Daryl. A petroleum engineer by trade, he retired from an oil company at age sixty and looked forward to playing golf all day, every day.

Within six months, he was bored silly. And before long, he was driving his wife Vicki crazy. Then one day he stumbled upon an open house for a place that "needed work."

The next morning he turned up at my office with a plan. "The house is going for $350,000," he told me. "I think it needs about $45,000 worth of renovations. What do you think about me buying this place and fixing it up? Based on what the neighbourhood is like and what homes there are going for, I bet I could sell it for about $500,000."

I trusted Daryl's estimate because he had lived in the neighbourhood for twenty years. But I still had a question. "Who's going to do the work?" I asked.

"Vicki and I will. We think it will be fun."

I told Daryl my story of how much "fun" I'd had fixing up my house, but Daryl wasn't put off. "This is something I've always wanted to do," he said. "We're gonna give it a shot."

Long story short, Daryl and Vicki not only did most of the work themselves, but they got it done in less than four months, after which they resold the property for $485,000. That was a little less than the $500,000 Daryl had hoped to get for the place, and their fix-up costs totaled around $55,000, about 20 percent more than Daryl originally figured. Still, after paying the real estate agent's commission on the sale, they still managed to clear more than $50,000 in profit!

After that, Daryl was hooked. He's now gone the fixer-upper route four times in the last six years. And he's not only having fun, he's also making money—so much that he hasn't had to tap into his retirement nest egg.

HOW TO EVALUATE A FIXER-UPPER

Fixer-uppers come in two basic categories: There are cosmetic fixer-uppers and then there are structural fixer-uppers.

A cosmetic fixer upper is a home that merely needs to be freshened up. The work required may be as simple as buffing out hardwood floors or clearing the yard and laying down new sod. At most, it may involve putting new fronts on the kitchen cabinets. Cosmetic fixes are almost always cheaper and easier to do than structural ones.

Structural fixes are exactly what they sound like. They involve the big stuff, such as roofing, wiring, plumbing, or foundations, which generally means a lot of work and a good-size bill. The good news is that problems like these can be so expensive or difficult to fix that you can almost always get a really good deal on houses that suffer from them.

In either case, before you take on a fixer-upper, make sure you know the facts. Get at least three first-rate contractors to give you estimates of what they think the work will cost and how long it will take. Then add 50 percent and ask yourself if you really have the time and money to take on the project.

3 SECRETS TO SUCCESSFUL FIXER-UPPERS

1. **Don't buy a fixer-upper in a neighbourhood filled with them.** The secret to making real money in this game is to buy a fixer-upper in the nicest area you can afford. You want a property that's at the low end of prices in the neighbourhood, not the high end. To put it bluntly, it should be the worst house on the best block.

2. **Ask your lender about special home-improvement loans.** Some companies now offer what are called "renovation loans" or "purchase and renovate loans"— mortgages that finance both the purchase of a house and the cost of fixing it up.

3. **Make sure you leave yourself room for upside!** Don't expect to sell a fixer-upper for a profit unless you're able to buy it at a bargain price. What this means is that you should consider only fixer-upper properties that are at least 20 percent below prevailing market prices.

STEP EIGHT: CONSIDER BUYING A TWO-FAMILY HOME

This is a great option for would-be homebuyers whose income is erratic, uncertain, or just too small to cover the costs of owning a home. The idea is simple: You live in one of the apartments, rent out the other one—and use the proceeds to cover part or all of your mortgage payments and other expenses.

You may think, "I could never afford a two-family home." But you might be wrong. Often, the rent from one unit can help you pay for a huge portion of your mortgage. I have friends who live in the upper level of a duplex they own, and the rent they get from the lower unit practically covers their monthly payment for the entire building. In other words, they live almost for free.

When you buy a two-family home with the idea of renting out one of the units, what counts is the cash flow it can generate. As long as you can charge enough rent to cover your expenses, it doesn't really matter what the total costs are.

What does matter is being comfortable with the responsibilities that go along with being a landlord. You're the one who is going to be called when a pipe breaks at two in the morning. That said, dealing with tenants doesn't have to be a nightmare. The trick is being selective about who you rent to. There are entire books written about just this issue. But the long and the short of it is that you can't discriminate based on race, religion, age, or gender. What you can do is make sure that your potential tenants are reliable. You can check their credit history (get their permission and have them pay for it) and request references from former landlords and current employers. Best of all, you can hire a property management company do all of this work for you.

STEP NINE: FIND OUT WHAT COMPARABLE PROPERTIES ARE SELLING FOR

One of the things that can make buying real estate complicated is that it's often hard to figure out what a particular house is really worth.

There's only one way to know for sure. That's to "run the comps"—to research what comparable houses in the same neighbourhood have been selling for. Any good real estate agent will be able to do this for you at no cost.

You should run the comps even if you "know the neighbourhood." Thinking you know what prices are and actually knowing them are two different things. Your purchase decision should be based on hard facts, not hunches.

STEP TEN: MAKE AN OFFER

If you're not scared when you make an offer on a home, you are definitely the exception, not the rule. Most people get really nervous when they make an offer on a property. There are so many factors to consider—and so much money at stake—that pulling the trigger can be downright nerve wracking.

Having purchased three properties in the last three years, I can tell you that it does get easier the more you do it. But that doesn't mean it's ever really easy.

I certainly understand what it's like to freeze up and not be able to make a decision. Back in the mid-1990s, I found myself unable to pull the trigger for nearly four years!

It began when my friend Andrew and I were finally able to rent out the suburban fixer-upper we owned for enough money to cover our mortgage. I was more than ready to move into San Francisco, but I wasn't comfortable yet with the prices there, so I rented an apartment in the Marina district for $1,250 a month. Before long, I realized renting was silly, and I asked my landlord if she would be interested in selling her building to me. It was a small building, consisting of just two one-bedroom apartments, and I figured it couldn't be that expensive.

As it turned out, my landlord was interested in selling, but she wanted $500,000 for the building. My little apartment, she said, was worth $250,000.

I thought that was crazy. So instead of buying, I became a "professional open house looker" on weekends. Over the next few months, I looked and looked and looked at homes in the Marina. Pretty soon, I was very knowledgeable about the local real estate market. I knew what was selling and what wasn't. I could tell almost immediately if a house was priced right. I also got to know the local real estate agents, because I talked to them at the open houses I visited.

Unfortunately, I didn't make any offers. Two years passed, and now my apartment, which I could have bought for

$250,000 when I first moved in, was worth closer to $350,000. The building that I had been offered for $500,000 was now worth around $750,000!

Had I learned anything?

Of course not. Once again, I thought it was crazy. "The market has to drop!" I told myself, and did nothing.

KNOWLEDGE WITHOUT OFFERS COSTS MONEY

By the time I bought, I had wasted four years looking! As a result, I wound up paying $640,000 for a two-bedroom condo that I probably could have bought for about $300,000 when I first moved to the Marina. Of course, I was able to make a nice profit when I sold it for $900,000 less than four years later. But if I'd bought it when I should have, I would have made twice as much.

My paralysis cost me a lot of money. If I had to do it all over again, I would have run the comps and made an offer the moment my landlord told me she was willing to sell.

Learn from my lesson. Follow the steps I've laid out in this chapter and start looking at properties. Spend a few weekends (maybe even a month) going to open houses. But then STOP LOOKING AND MAKE AN OFFER.

The biggest mistakes I've made in real estate haven't been what I've bought—but what I didn't buy when I had the chance. It's the offers you don't make that wind up costing you the most money.

STEP ELEVEN:
BE PREPARED TO CLOSE

When you make that offer on a house and then get the great news that it's been accepted, you're not home free. You still have to close on the purchase, and this can be a complicated process that takes weeks if not months. Here are three things you can do to make sure the closing process goes as smoothly and quickly as possible. Your real estate agent should be able to assist you with all of these.

1. **Order up a home inspection—and attend it yourself.** Unless you are purchasing a new, custom-built property, you should never close on a house without having it first checked out by a professional home inspector. You should be able to get a referral from your real estate agent or your mortgage advisor—preferably from both. And make sure the inspector is a member of the Canadian Association of Home and Property Inspectors (**www.cahi.ca**). A properly performed home inspection is essential, since it will uncover any serious problems involving structural issues, leaks, faulty appliances, electrical and plumbing woes, and so on. (You might also consider ordering up a termite inspection and, if the property has water tanks or a well, a water inspection, too.)

   A pre-purchase inspection for a 165 to 205 m² (1,800 to 2,200 sq. ft.) home typically takes about three hours and costs under $500. Following the inspection, the buyer is presented with a written report, consolidating the details of the inspection. The home inspector should be willing to answer any questions a buyer might have and to clarify the limitations of the inspection to avoid misunderstandings.

Although a professional inspector will provide you with a written report of his findings, don't just wait for him to submit it. Show up at the house and personally watch him conduct the inspection. If you have a real estate agent (and you should), make sure he or she also attends. It would be nice to think all home inspectors are created equal but they are not. *Chances are yours will do a better job if he knows you are looking over his shoulder.*

You can get some good information on home inspections from Canada Mortgage and Housing Corporation (**www.cmhc-schl.gc.ca**).

2. **Arrange to get homeowner's insurance.** As I mentioned in Chapter Six, most lenders require you to have homeowner's coverage before you close, so you should get going on this now. The homeowner's policy should protect you from loss caused by fire, weather damage, burglary, and so on. If you live in a flood zone, you may need a separate policy to cover that possibility. If you're buying a condo, find out what type of coverage the building has and what you'll need to get for yourself.

WEBSITES TO HELP YOU FIND A GOOD DEAL ON INSURANCE	
EDUCATIONAL SITES	**SHOPPING SITES**
www.ibc.ca	www.allstate.ca
www.insurance-canada.ca	www.kanetix.ca
	www.canadalife.ca

3. **Alert your lender.** Even though you've been pre-approved for a mortgage, that doesn't mean you can assume it's a done deal. For one thing, the lender has to appraise the house you're buying to confirm its value. For another, there are all kinds of extremely important—and potentially expensive—details like closing costs that must be settled. (We'll cover these later on in this chapter.) The sooner your lender gets started processing all this, the sooner you will be able to close.

STEP TWELVE: GIVE YOURSELF A DEADLINE—AND PUT IT IN WRITING

I'm a big believer in "dreams with deadlines." If you really want to buy a home, then one of the most important things you can do to make that dream come true is to set a deadline for yourself.

Below is what I call the *Automatic Millionaire Homeowner Promise*. Please get a pen and fill it out right now. This may seem silly, but trust me—I've seen firsthand how effective this kind of exercise can be to really get you moving.

There will be some people who read this book and complain that it's too late for them to buy a home, much less get rich in real estate. They will have bought this book to fulfill a dream, but they won't do anything with it.

Then there will be people who read it and then take action! Be one of them. Let others keep wishing and hoping. Become a doer who gets things done. And do it right now—this minute! **Make a commitment—and sign it!**

THE AUTOMATIC MILLIONAIRE HOMEOWNER PROMISE

I, _____ (insert name), know I deserve to own a home, and I know I can do it.

I promise myself that I will get my mortgage pre-approved by _____ (insert date).

I hereby promise myself that starting on _____ (insert date), I will begin going to open houses.

I will make an offer on a property by no later than _____ (insert date).

I promise myself that I will be a homeowner by _____ (insert date).

Signed: _____

SO YOUR MORTGAGE
HAS BEEN APPROVED:
HOW TO SURVIVE THE CLOSING

It's always exciting when your mortgage advisor calls to say that the lender has checked out the house you want to buy and given your pre-approved mortgage the final and official okay. But don't break out the champagne just yet. There are a number of things you need to do to make sure your interests are fully protected.

To begin with, you should carefully review the terms of your new mortgage with your banker or broker. Are the term, the interest rate, the amortization and ALL the other conditions (such as portability, prepayment options, and so forth) exactly what you were told they would be? If not, insist on getting a full explanation of what has changed and why.

You should also ask your lawyer for details of the taxes and disbursements associated with your mortgage. Most of these costs will be covered by the mortgage loan itself, but you should still check with your lawyer to identify any outstanding details.

Congratulations! You now know how to find and buy yourself a home—the smart way. Next, I'm going to let you in on a secret to making this process even less stressful and more enjoyable.

AUTOMATIC MILLIONAIRE HOMEOWNER ACTION STEPS

Reviewing the actions we laid out in this chapter, here's what you should be doing right now to find yourself a home to buy.

❑ Complete and sign The Automatic Millionaire Homeowner Promise.

❑ If you're renting, see if your landlord is willing to sell.

❑ Figure out what kind of home you want to buy.

❑ Create a target market and start going to open houses in that area.

❑ Consider new developments, fixer-uppers, or two-family homes.

❑ When you find a house you like, "run the comps" and make an offer!

❑ Notify your lender and prepare to close.

CHAPTER EIGHT

HOW TO HIRE
A GREAT
REAL ESTATE
COACH

Let's be honest. Even with everything you've learned about becoming an Automatic Millionaire Homeowner, buying and selling homes can still be a stressful business. There's a lot to do and a lot to know.

Fortunately, there's a simple way to make the process easier and even enjoyable. What you need to do is get yourself a licensed professional real estate agent. A great real estate agent can be the coach you need to make your home-buying experience both enjoyable and profitable.

This is exactly what John and Lucy Martin did. Throughout it all, from the Martins' first starter home to their most recent dream house, real estate agents guided them along the path to smart homeownership—which ultimately led them to become Automatic Millionaire Homeowners. And real estate agents have done the same thing for me. Like the Martins, I've used real estate agents in every one of my real estate transactions, both buying and selling. The value these professionals have given me over the years has both saved and made me a fortune.

Now it's your turn. This chapter is designed to teach you exactly what a good real estate agent does and how to find a great one. It won't take you long to read, but it could make the difference between a journey that's fun and profitable and one that's stressful and unproductive.

EIGHT IMPORTANT THINGS A GREAT REAL ESTATE AGENT CAN DO FOR YOU

Before I became a financial advisor, I was a real estate agent (specializing in commercial properties) and I've worked with real estate agents on all of my real estate transactions. I know personally how much they can help you. But I also know that not all real estate agents are created equal. There are more than 100,000 real estate agents in Canada, with more entering the profession every day. There are full-time agents and those who work part time. Many are great—but not all. So how do you find the one who can make you money and make your life easier during the homebuying process? Here's a list of things you should look for:

1. **A great real estate agent will listen to you carefully.** Great agents are great listeners. They have to be in order to really help you. When a great agent meets with you for the first time, he or she will pepper you with questions to find out what you're looking for, what you really want, why you want it, and most important, what you think you can afford.

2. **A great real estate agent will help you figure out what you really can afford.** As I've discussed before, when it comes to buying a home, there is generally a big difference between what you think you can afford and what you REALLY can afford. If you haven't already followed my advice to get yourself pre-approved for a mortgage, the first thing a top-notch agent will do is help you determine approximately how much house you are realistically going to be able to buy. At the very least, he or she will run your numbers and at least give you a "ballpark" estimate of what your price range should be. She will know which developments accept low- or no-down payment financing and which developments insist on 25 percent. A great agent will also provide you with referrals to at least three bankers or brokers who can help you get preapproved for an exact mortgage amount.

3. **A great real estate agent will save you time by narrowing your search.** Finding the right house in the right location at the right price is not easy. A great agent will help you figure out what exactly you are looking for—

and then whittle down the possibilities to manageable proportions. Among other things, he or she will take advantage of what's called the Multiple Listing Service (or MLS), a searchable, computerized directory of what's for sale that is available in its entirety only to licensed professionals. (You can visit the MLS website at **www.mls.ca**). A great agent won't run you ragged (and waste your time) by dragging you around to countless properties. Rather, the agent will show you a selection online, allowing you to narrow your choices before you actually hit the streets. He or she will then "tour you" to ones you've chosen—and keep track of what you like.

4. **A great real estate agent will educate you about the market.** Great real estate agents know more than simply what's for sale in a particular neighbourhood. They know the neighbourhood. They can tell you all about an area's history, what makes it special, and where they see the market there going. If you're looking at a new development, the agent can share with you what he or she knows about the developer's track record and plans for the future.

5. **A great real estate agent will help you determine what price to offer for a property you want to buy—and how to evaluate a purchase offer when you're selling.** Once you find something you like, you're going to have to make an offer. If you're selling a property, you're

going to have to decide whether to accept or reject the offers you receive. To make smart choices, you'll need a lot of information quickly. A great agent will get you that information. Perhaps most important, he or she will "run comps" for you—provide you with an analysis of what comparable properties in the area have been selling for.

6. A great real estate agent will show you ways to get more value from the property. From the moment a great real estate agent first sees a property, he or she is thinking about what could be done to increase its value. Install new cabinets in the kitchen, pull up the rugs, redo the hardwood floors, take down this wall, knock out the back bedroom and add a master bath—great agents will look at property and immediately begin suggesting ways you could make it more attractive and valuable. They can also refer you to reliable contractors who can turn those suggestions into reality. And they can help you "stage" a home that you're getting ready to sell—in essence, setting up the home to look its best for potential buyers.

7. A great real estate agent will hold your hand at closing. The closing of a home purchase can often be a scary few hours. A good agent will make sure you are thoroughly prepared. If you ask them, great agents will go over the paperwork with you and your lawyer, checking it for

errors. They will also work closely with you and your banker or mortgage broker to make sure your loan looks the way it should.

8. **When you're selling a house, a great real estate agent will market the property aggressively.** When you decide to sell a house, a great agent will handle all the marketing efforts. In addition to helping you ready the property for sale by "staging it," these efforts may include preparing sales brochures or flyers; running advertisements in newspapers, real estate magazines, and online; getting the property listed on the MLS; and holding open houses for both real estate agents and the public.

HOW IS A REAL ESTATE AGENT PAID?

Real estate agents are almost always paid by commission—meaning that when a sale closes, they get a percentage of the purchase price (usually 6 percent). In other words, if the house sells for $200,000, the buyer's agent and the seller's agent (also known as the listing agent) are entitled to a commission of $12,000. Generally speaking, they split the commission 50/50. This commission is usually deducted from the proceeds of the sale—which is to say, *it is paid by the seller.*

IF YOU'RE SELLING, KEEP IN MIND THAT COMMISSIONS MAY BE NEGOTIABLE

If you're looking for an agent to help you *sell* a property, keep in mind that depending on the market, commissions may be negotiable. Real estate agents may give discounts to sellers who plan to buy another home with the proceeds from the sale—on the assumption that they'll be handling the purchase as well. So if that's what you're doing, make sure to ask. Also, if the market is really hot and properties are flying, a real estate agent may be willing to discount her commission because she knows the property will move quickly and not take a lot of time to sell. (On the other hand, if the market is slow or you insist on asking too high a price for your property, a smart real estate agent will not likely give you a break.)

A discounted commission may drop the standard commission from 6 percent to 5.5 percent or even 5 percent. That may not sound like much, but if you can get a 6 percent fee cut to 5 percent, you'll save yourself $2,000 on the sale of a $200,000 home.

AND NOW THERE'S SOMETHING CALLED THE BONUS COMMISSION

When real estate sales slow or there is a glut of properties similar to your home on the market in your neighbourhood, it may take longer to sell your home. A great way to get a property to stand out and sell faster is to offer your agent a bonus commission. Instead of the standard 6 percent, you might offer a commission of 7 percent or 8 percent—provided they can find a buyer for your house within a certain amount of time or who's willing to pay above a certain price. This is not unheard of—and it can work like a charm. In Manhattan, where I live, creative sellers are even offering agents plasma-screen televisions, trips to Hawaii, and (in a few cases) cars as incentives to sell their places fast and for higher prices.

Whatever the commission winds up being, you should know that your real estate agent usually doesn't get to keep all of it. The agent usually has to split some of the commission with the brokerage company the agent works for, and he or she also has to pay for the costs associated with marketing the property. The fact is that most real estate agents really end up really earning their commission. It's not an easy business.

IT'S IMPORTANT TO KNOW
WHOM YOUR AGENT REPRESENTS

Unless you have an agreement to the contrary, real estate agents represent the seller of a property. If you're a buyer, this is not something I would recommend, since when you're buying a house, you want to be represented by someone who has your interests at heart and no one else's.

One way to make sure this is the case is to get in writing

upfront that in any and all deals, your real estate agent will be representing you and you alone. If you're a buyer, you can do this with what is called a "buyer's agreement"—basically a contract in which the agent agrees that he or she will look out for your best interests and represents only you, not the seller. A buyer's agent is responsible not just for driving a good bargain, but also for providing you with a complete picture of your new property

In return, the agent may ask you to promise to work with him or her exclusively (as opposed to improving your odds of finding a good deal by working with several different agents at the same time). If you are willing to sign an exclusive buyer's agreement, I recommend limiting your commitment to no more than sixty days—thirty would be even better because it will motivate your agent to work hard and fast for you.

THE TRICKY PART OF
WHO WORKS FOR WHOM

Occasionally, a real estate agent will show you a house that is represented by another agent at his or her firm. Technically speaking, you now have a dual agent, representing both the buyer and the seller.

As with any other agent with whom you have no contract, a dual agent is under no obligation to tell you anything about the seller's property. But he or she must disclose information about you that's of interest to the seller.

FREE AUDIO BONUS!

HOW TO HIRE A GREAT REAL ESTATE AGENT

At the beginning of this chapter, I said you shouldn't hire just any real estate agent but a great one! What distinguishes many real estate agents who are serious about their careers is membership in the **Canadian Real Estate Association (CREA)**. Their website can be found at **www.crea.ca**. You should also look for designations like FRI or FRI(E), which stand for Fellow of the Real Estate Institute and Fellow of the Real Estate Institute (Executive). The REI conducts courses and continuing education programs and also grants the Certified Real Estate Specialist (CRES) designation

For more information about real estate agents and brokers how to find a good one—you can listen to a powerful interview I did with a senior real estate executive and economist, David Lereah. Just go to my website at **www.finishrich.com** and visit the Automatic Millionaire Homeowner resource center. This interview is loaded with great tips—and it's my free gift to you! Also visit **www.mls.ca** for great information about how to find both a real estate agent and a home.

THREE BASIC RULES FOR HIRING A
GREAT REAL ESTATE AGENT

As with anything else, hiring a great real estate agent is a matter of common sense and good judgment. Follow these three basic rules and you shouldn't go wrong.

RULE NO. 1:
GET A RECOMMENDATION

When you're ready to hire a real estate agent, don't be shy. Ask your friends, relatives, coworkers, and neighbours whom they used the last time they bought or sold a home. Your goal should be to get at least three referrals, so you can compare a number of real estate agents before you decide to work with one.

RULE NO. 2:
IF YOU CAN'T GET A REFERRAL
TO AN AGENT YOU LIKE,
DON'T GIVE UP

Referrals are great, but they are not essential. It may be a little more challenging, but it is definitely not impossible to find a good agent on your own. Unless you live in the middle of nowhere, I'll bet at least a half dozen real estate brokerage firms have local offices in your neighbourhood. Call three of them, ask for the manager, and tell him or her that you're looking for an experienced agent who specializes in working with someone like you.

In addition to "cold calling" real estate agencies, you can also do a little investigating on your own. I'm a big believer in the idea that success leaves clues. If you are looking for a house in a specific neighbourhood, an incredibly easy way to find a top agent is simply to drive around the area looking for "For Sale" signs in front yards. When you see one, write down the name of the agent on it, and make a note of whose name you see the most. The agent with the most listings is usually an expert on that neighbourhood. That's the person you probably want.

RULE NO. 3:
INTERVIEW, INTERVIEW, INTERVIEW

Don't make assumptions or take someone else's word for it. Even if an agent looks great on paper (and even if he or she has been recommended by your oldest and best friend), don't decide to work with anyone until you've sat down and conducted a long, searching interview.

When you meet with a real estate agent, I highly recommend that you ask the following questions.

- How long have you been in the business?
- How long have you worked in this particular market?
- How many listings (properties for sale where you represent the seller) do you have?
- How many clients are you currently working with?

- How many deals did you do last year in the area I'm interested in?
- Why should I work with you rather than one of your competitors?
- What makes you a good real estate agent?
- What is your process—how do you work with your clients?
- Do you have a team or an assistant? Will I be working with them or with you?
- Can you give me the names of three clients you've worked with whose situation was similar to mine?

These questions can quickly weed out an agent who's not for you. When I first moved to New York, I was referred by a friend to an agent he really liked—but within minutes, I knew the agent wasn't right for me. How did I know that? When I asked him how many lofts had he sold or helped someone buy over the last year in the neighbourhoods I was interested in, he said the answer was none! So I thanked him for his time—and continued my search for a top agent.

MAKE A COMMITMENT

You now know more about what real estate agents do than 90 percent of the people who will ever buy or sell a home. In short, you are ready to get going. So right now, this very minute, make a commitment to yourself to go out and interview a real estate agent.

My hunch is that in no time you'll have a fantastic real estate agent on your side acting as your advocate and coach to help you find the right home for you.

Now that you're really ready to buy, I'm going to share with you a really simple system called an automatic biweekly mortgage payment plan that could save you tens of thousands of dollars in interest payments (maybe more) and shave up to seven years off the time it will take you to pay off your mortgage.

AUTOMATIC MILLIONAIRE HOMEOWNER ACTION STEPS

Reviewing the actions we laid out in this chapter, here's what you should be doing right now to find a great real estate agent you can trust.

- ❑ Make a commitment to go out and find yourself a top real estate agent.

- ❑ Ask everyone you know who has ever bought or sold a home whether they would recommend the real estate agent they used.

- ❑ "Cold call" local real estate brokerages and research local sales to compile a list of agents worth considering.

- ❑ Schedule interviews with the top three prospects and make a decision.

- ❑ Visit **www.finishrich.com/homeowner** and listen to my interview with David Lereah on how to hire a great real estate agent.

CHAPTER NINE

MAKE YOUR
MORTGAGE
AUTOMATIC AND
SAVE $46,000
ON YOUR HOME

One of the most valuable secrets I've learned from my Automatic Millionaire friends like John and Lucy Martin—as well as the original Automatic Millionaires, Jim and Sue McIntyre—is the power of paying your mortgage off early by splitting your monthly payment into two biweekly payments.

In *The Automatic Millionaire*, I laid out a simple system that any homeowner can use to pay off a twenty-five-year mortgage as much as seven years early . . . *automatically*. I shared this message on *The Oprah Winfrey Show*, and viewers were simply blown away by how easy this was. After my appearance, our phones rang off the hook. "How can that be?" people wanted to know. "It can't be that easy to save so much money on a mortgage. What's the trick?"

Well, in truth, it's not a trick.

Think about it this way. The problem with a twenty-five-year mortgage is that it's designed to make you spend twenty-five years paying it off! Say you buy a home with a $200,000 mortgage at 7 percent. If you take the full twenty-five years to pay it off, you will wind up actually giving the bank about $420,000, since in addition to paying back the principal, you will also pay more than $220,240 in interest.

What's a better approach? Well, if you were to take that same mortgage and make the payments on a biweekly instead of a monthly schedule, you would cut the total payment time by about five years—and in the process save yourself more than $45,000 in interest payments.

Want to see how easy this is?

PAY YOUR MORTGAGE FASTER— PAINLESSLY

Here's how it works. All you do is take the normal twenty-five-year mortgage you have and instead of making the monthly payment the way you normally do, you split it down the middle and pay half every two weeks.

Say your mortgage payment is $2,000 a month. Under my biweekly plan, instead of paying $2,000 to your mortgage lender once every month, you would pay $1,000 every two weeks. At the beginning, paying $1,000 every two weeks probably won't feel any different than paying $2,000 once a month. But as anyone who's ever looked at a calendar can tell you, it's hardly the same thing. A month, after all, is a little longer than four weeks. And so what happens as a result of switching to a biweekly payment plan is that over the course of a year you gradually get further and further ahead in your payments, until by the end of the year you have paid the equivalent of not twelve but thirteen monthly payments. Best of all, because it's so gradual, you'll hardly feel the pinch.

The math is actually quite simple. A monthly mortgage payment of $2,000 amounts to $24,000 a year. But when you make a half payment every two weeks instead of a full one once a month, you end up making twenty-six half payments over the course of a year. That's twenty-six payments of $1,000—for a total of $26,000, or one extra month's worth of payments, painlessly.

WHAT COULD YOU DO WITH AN EXTRA $45,000?

The impact of that extra month's payment is awesome. Depending on your interest rate, you will end up paying off a twenty-five-year mortgage about five years early, and a fifteen-year mortgage two years early! You will be debt-free years ahead of schedule, saving you thousands of dollars in interest payments over the life of your loan.

I'm not just making these figures up. Check out the table that follows. It shows the difference between a monthly and a biweekly payment plan for a $200,000 twenty-five-year mortgage with an interest rate of 7 percent.

(For simplicity, I haven't included a term for the mortgage, and I'm assuming the interest rate stays the same. Remember, interest rates may change from term to term. If you lock in to a five-year fixed-rate mortgage, for example, interest rates may have risen or fallen when the five-year period ends. But your amortization period remains the same unless you negotiate a new one.)

The monthly pay-off schedule winds up incurring a total of $220,250 in interest charges over the life of the loan. The biweekly schedule, on the other hand, runs up just $172,800 in interest. In other words, switching to the biweekly plan will save you more than $47,000.

MONTHLY VS. BIWEEKLY VS. WEEKLY PAYMENTS				
Principal = **$200,000** Interest Rate = **7.00%** Amortization = **25** years				
Payment Schedule	$/Payment	Total Interest	Interest Savings	Payoff Period
monthly	$1,400	$220,250	none	25 years
biweekly	$700	$172,800	$47,450	20.46 years
weekly	$350	$172,270	$47,980	20.42 years

If you'd like to figure out how much you could save on your own mortgage, go online and visit one of the many mortgage calculators provided by Canada's banks, trust companies, mortgage brokers and others. (You'll find one at **www.scotiabank.com**, for example, and another at **www.tdcanadatrust.com/mortgages**.) You can then plug in your own numbers and quickly see how much you could save by switching to a biweekly or even a weekly payment plan.

ALL IT TAKES IS TEN MINUTES

The great thing about switching to a biweekly payment plan is that it allows you to save money over the long run without refinancing or otherwise changing your mortgage. All it takes is one call.

That's because these days most mortgage lenders offer programs designed to totally automate the process I've just described. To enroll, all you need to do is phone your lender or go online to its website.

Remember, this does not mean that you are refinancing or changing your mortgage. All it means is that you are interested in signing up to pay off your mortgage in a slightly different manner—namely, one that will allow you to make your mortgage payments on a biweekly basis.

WHY NOT DO IT YOURSELF?

You could easily use your bank's online automatic bill-paying service to schedule biweekly mortagage payments for yourself.

Depending on the features of your mortgage, you could add 10 percent to your regular mortgage payment each month and have the money applied towards the principal. Or you could make one extra payment at the end of the year and again have it go toward your principal. But note that word "could." Let's face it—some things are much easier said than done. Just like most people won't save if they don't Make It Automatic—in the real world, most people won't make extra mortgage payments unless they Make It Automatic.

If you decide to do it yourself, my suggestion is that you add an extra 10 percent a month towards your mortgage payment—*and make the payment automatic.*

RICHER, FASTER!

A biweekly payment plan does more than allow you to pay off your home early. It also makes it easier to manage your money, since most of us get paid every two weeks. You'll be richer faster, with a plan that makes your life easier. So consider it. You're on your way to becoming an Automatic Millionaire Homeowner.

AUTOMATIC MILLIONAIRE HOMEOWNER ACTION STEPS

Reviewing the actions we laid out in this chapter, here's what you should be doing right now to save yourself thousands of dollars by setting up an Automatic Biweekly Mortgage Payment Plan.

❑ Check out the calculator at **www.scotiabank.com** to see how much time and money you could save by paying off your mortgage biweekly.

❑ Call your lender to get more information about its biweekly payment plan.

❑ Sign up for the plan.

CHAPTER TEN

FROM ORDINARY HOMEOWNER TO AUTOMATIC MILLIONAIRE HOMEOWNER

By now you know more about the fundamentals of buying a house than 90 percent of all homeowners. And for those of you who have already used this knowledge to buy yourself your first home—congratulations! You are well on your way to a lifetime of financial security. But it need not stop there. In this chapter, I will show you how you can turn your home—your little gold mine—into a gold rush!

The key to transforming yourself from an ordinary homeowner to an Automatic Millionaire Homeowner is to learn how to use your new home to build yet more wealth. Whether you already own your home or you are about to take the plunge, your model should be John and Lucy Martin, who used the equity in their first home as the foundation for a lifetime of financial security.

DOING IT AGAIN—ONLY BETTER

The single most important thing the Martins did after deciding to become homeowners was actually something they didn't do. THEY DIDN'T SELL THEIR FIRST HOME. This was also true of the original Automatic Millionaires, Jim and Sue McIntyre, whom I wrote about in *The Automatic Millionaire*. For both of these couples, this smart but not obvious decision wound up having a profound impact on their ability to accumulate wealth.

In both cases, after living in their first homes for a while and building up some equity, these perfectly ordinary people earning a perfectly ordinary income didn't simply sell out and buy a bigger house. Instead, they rented out their first home, used the rental income to cover the mortgage payments on it, and borrowed against the equity they'd built up to purchase a new home to live in.

To do this, they had to adopt what I call the Automatic Millionaire Homeowner Mindset. This is a different way of thinking about your house. Most people think of their house simply as a place to live. The Martins and McIntyres thought of their homes as places to live but also as *vehicles for building wealth*.

BIGGER IS NOT ALWAYS BETTER

The Martins and the McIntyres didn't do what most people do. Most people buy a starter house and then, as their family grows, they sell it and use the proceeds to buy a bigger house. Usually much bigger. This leads to bigger mortgage payments. Usually much bigger. In most cases, it's why very few people ultimately own more than one house at a time.

How could the Martins, who never earned a big income, afford to own two houses at the same time? It's simple. Unlike most people, who are stuck paying off their big mortgages by themselves, the Martins had tenants—and the rent they paid—to help them build equity.

If you go back and reread the story of the Martins, you'll see that when they bought their first home, their initial priority was to focus on paying down their mortgage early. And when their home went up in value, they didn't rush to cash out so they could buy a bigger house.

Remember what John Martin told me about what he and his wife did when they were ready to buy a second home that could accommodate their growing family: He said they had to stretch to make the purchase, but they didn't stretch too much. "In fact," he said, "we actually stretched a little *less* than we could afford because we had decided not to sell our first house but, instead, to keep it and rent it out. So instead of cashing out completely, all we did was refinance the house just enough to pull out a down payment on our new place."

You can do the exact same thing. Here's how.

WILL YOUR HOME GENERATE
POSITIVE CASH FLOW?

Often, you don't have to live in your home all that long before it's capable of generating positive cash flow. If the real estate market goes up over five years and homes become more expensive in your area, in most cases rents will go up also. There are exceptions to this rule because every market is different, but it's usually the case that if housing prices go up, so do rents.

Check right now to see if rents in your area are high enough to cover the costs you'd incur if you were to rent out your place. Pull out the local newspaper and look at the rental ads, or have a real estate agent who specializes in rentals come over and evaluate your home.

Keep in mind that figuring out how much it would cost you to turn your house into a rental property involves more than just adding up your current mortgage payment and your property tax bill. You also need to figure in maintenance (the cost of everything from fixing leaky faucets to replacing balky furnaces) as well as extra insurance premiums and an allowance for vacancies and bad debts.

If it turns out that it would indeed be possible for you to charge enough rent for your place to cover all these costs, you need to ask yourself an important question: Are you ready to get into the landlord business? If you are, it may be time to consider getting a tenant for your current house and buying another for yourself.

BEING A LANDLORD IS EASIER THAN YOU THINK

Keep in mind that renting out a home can be easier than you think. You can hire a real estate agent to list it and a property management company to manage it. (Your real estate agent should be able to recommend a management company. Figure on paying them between 6 percent and 12 percent of your rental income.) Or you can do it all yourself.

The point is that managing one rental home doesn't have to be a big deal—but it can lead to great wealth over time, as someone else pays off your mortgage.

If becoming a landlord is such a good deal, why aren't lots of homeowners doing it? In fact, they are. There are nearly 4 million rental units in Canada, according to CMHC figures. Almost 2 million of them are owned by "small investors" like you and me.

THE PROS AND CONS OF BEING A LANDLORD

Before we go into the details of renting your home, I have to mention a couple of disadvantages that you should consider before you decide to become a landlord in Canada. First, many investors in rental housing complain about high property taxes. (Well, who doesn't complain about taxes?) They also complain about government interference in the rental market.

Each province in Canada has different regulations in place that affect rental housing. Some provinces control the amount that a landlord can add to the monthly rent. Other provinces impose rules on the way landlords can charge tenants for security deposits. You should make sure that you understand how these regulations might affect you before you decide to become a landlord.

I still think being a landlord is a great way to increase your wealth. You just have to be smart about it.

YOUR TENANTS CAN PAY YOU TWICE

In some cases, you may be able to rent out your first house for enough money to cover not only all the costs of owning the property but also to cover some or all of the mortgage on your second home. This is what happened with the Martins, and it's an option for me right now.

As I write this in 2005, housing prices in New York City are through the roof. Our loft is worth at least $1 million more than I paid for it three years ago. What's more, rents have gone up to the point where we could rent it out right now for about $5,000 more a month than it currently costs us in mortgage payments and other costs. That's $60,000 a year in positive cash flow. Not bad.

I'm also currently in the process of buying a new condo in a building still under construction in the currently trendy Brooklyn neighbourhood of Williamsburg. The price of this condo was $700,000, and it's already worth close to $1,000,000.

When I close, I will probably make a cash down payment of around $140,000, or around 20 percent of the purchase price. Depending on the mortgage I get, my monthly payments will be between $3,000 and $5,000.

I had originally thought of this place as an investment property I could rent out. But if my wife and I wanted to, we could rent out our loft now for enough to cover its mortgage *and* generate sufficient positive cash flow to pay the mortgage on the Williamsburg condo, and maybe the maintenance, taxes, and insurance as well—meaning we could basically live there for free.

This is what is so much fun about real estate. It gives you so many options.

YOU REALLY CAN DO THIS, AND HERE'S HOW

You can read these examples and get skeptical or jealous or get going! I know you want to get going. With this in mind, let's look at four strategies you can use to build wealth through homeownership.

> **STRATEGY NO. 1:**
> **USE YOUR HOME EQUITY TO**
> **BUY YOUR NEXT PROPERTY**

The equity you have in your home is an asset. It belongs to you, not the bank. If you take out a $200,000 mortgage to buy a home for $250,000 and the property's value rises to $400,000, the $150,000 increase is yours, not the bank's. You've now got $200,000 in equity. You can use it or you can let it sit there. The choice is yours.

What you need to know about home equity is this: Right now, most people have more equity in their homes than they realize. Even with all those "no down payment" mortgages and over-ambitious purchases where people buy more house than they should, the huge run-up in real estate values since the mid-1990s has left most Canadians with a ton of equity in their houses. According to Canada Mortgage and Housing Corporation, Canadian homeowners have on average from $40,000 to $85,000 in equity in their homes. (The figure varies depending on whether the homeowner has a mortgage or not. Homeowners without a mortgage own their homes outright. The equity's all theirs!) But most people really don't appreciate or make good use of all this equity they own.

So how should you think about your home equity? There are at least three different ways. All are sensible, but only one of them—the third—will lead to your becoming an Automatic Millionaire Homeowner.

1. **As the ultimate safety net.** If you don't want to do anything risky, you can look at your home equity as a kind of forced savings account. You can pay off your mortgage early, as I suggested a few pages back, and when you're older, you'll be able to retire with no debt. Later, if you ever need money, there are a variety of ways to

make use of all the equity you have accumulated. The point is that you have a safety net—and options.

2. **As collateral for a loan.** Another way to take advantage of the equity in your current home is to arrange what is called a home-equity loan, in which the bank agrees to lend you the cash value of your equity. You should shop this loan just the way you would a regular mortgage to make sure you get a competitive rate. If your mortgage lender is a bank, it will likely provide a home-equity loan at the prime rate.

You can use a home equity loan for any reason—to pay for your kids' university, to start your own business, or to take a trip to Europe. But my recommendation is that you use your equity only to buy more assets, not to pay for daily living expenses, vacations, or credit card debt.

3. **As a stepping-stone to buy a second home.** This is how Automatic Millionaire Homeowners think about their home equity. You can see this mind-set at work in John and Lucy Martin's story. When they were ready to buy a second home, they did what is called a "cash-out refinance." It works like this: Say you bought a home with a $250,000 mortgage and the place is now worth $400,000. You could go to a bank or mortgage broker and refinance—that is, get a new mortgage to pay off the old one. Only now you would borrow not $250,000 but, say, $300,000. This would allow you to pay off the existing

$250,000 mortgage—and put $50,000 cash in your pocket. You then take that $50,000 and use it as a down payment on another home for you to live in while you rent out your first house.

Of course, you now owe more money ($300,000 instead of $250,000) and, depending on what type of new mortgage you get, your monthly payments may be higher—which is something you need to factor in when you're calculating whether the rent you think you can charge will cover all your costs.

In John and Lucy's case, their $30,000 starter house (remember, this was back in the 1960s) had increased in value to about $45,000 when they felt ready to buy their second home. They had already reduced their original mortgage balance to just $20,000, so they had no trouble getting a new $40,000 mortgage. That mortgage paid off the old one and left them with enough cash ($20,000) for a 20 percent down payment on the $100,000 home they had decided to buy. (Remember, the Martins lived in the U.S., where down payments are smaller than they usually are in Canada. Most lenders in Canada require a down payment of 25 percent for a conventional mortgage.) Eventually the Martins sold this second house—for $650,000—and moved to their dream home. By then, of course, they owned their first house free and clear. With the rent they earned from it over the years, they'd long since paid off its $40,000 mortgage and were now enjoying the positive cash flow it continued to generate—not to mention the phenomenal contribution to their net worth, as the house's value skyrocketed toward seven figures. They had become Automatic Homeowner Millionaires.

This is a classic example of how you can leverage your way to wealth. The Martins put $6,000 down on a starter home that within a few years was worth $45,000. (Keep in mind that even though the price of that house was $30,000, 80 percent of it was paid for with Other People's Money—namely, the mortgage they got from the bank.) The Martins then took $20,000 in cash out of the equity they had accumulated in that little house and used it as a down payment on a second house that they eventually sold for $650,000. And so on. Even adding in all the mortgage payments they made along the way, the amount of money they put in was only a small fraction of the wealth they came to own—especially when you count all the rent their tenants paid them over the years. That's the power of leverage. A small amount of cash at the beginning can put you in a position to reap huge asset values down the road.

STRATEGY NO. 2:
DOWNSIZE TO THE RIGHT SIZE

I covered this approach in Chapter Two, when I shared the story of my friends in Calgary, Rick and Molly. You'll find it on page 44. Reread it right now. Let it sink in. What this couple did is incredibly simple—yet most people don't do it. You could.

As I said earlier, what most people do when the value of their home goes up is to sell it and buy a bigger house with a bigger mortgage. The problem with this approach is that it doesn't make your life simpler. Rather, it usually makes it more expensive—more rooms to furnish, higher taxes to pay, richer neighbours to keep up with.

If you recall, the value of Rick and Molly's house jumped from $200,000 to $400,000 in just a few years. Now I know this is a best-case example, but how they decided to handle it demonstrates something important. Rather than simply sell their suddenly pricey home and use the windfall to buy a bigger house on a golf course with a bigger mortgage, they decided to use their equity to leverage their wealth and keep their life simple.

After they sold their house for $400,000, they took the $200,000 profit they made and used it to buy three new houses. First, they made a $75,000 down payment on what would be their new home—a $350,000 house in a community that was slightly less fancy than the one in which they had been living. They "downsized." This left them with a $275,000 mortgage, which at $1,650 a month, was only a little bit more than what they had been paying on their old place. Then they took the remaining $125,000 profit and used it to make down payments on two other $180,000 houses that they planned to use as rental properties. Because they were able to make such large down payments on these houses (around $75,000 each), the mortgage payments were relatively low (just $650 a month each) and they were easily able to rent them out for enough to generate positive cash flow from Day One. In fact, the extra cash the two rental properties threw off paid for the higher cost of the mortgage on their new home. So there they were, spending less than the

$1,300 a month it had cost them to live in their original $200,000 house—but now owning three homes worth more than $700,000!

Again, we see the power of leverage—making the same amount of money go five times as far.

This is probably the most straightforward approach to building wealth through homeownership. When your house goes up in value, you sell it and use part of the tax-free profits to put a down payment on a new house (with a new mortgage), and you put the rest of your profits in the bank. Then you wait until your new house appreciates and you do it again, and watch your bank balance grow.

Why is this such a phenomenally good deal? As I noted earlier, the government allows you to sell your home *without having to pay any taxes on the profits.* You simply have to have lived in the house you're selling as your principal residence.

To see how this works, let's use Rick and Molly as an example. Had they not wanted to be landlords, they could have taken their $200,000 in tax-free profits and used $60,000 of it for a 25 percent down payment on another $240,000 house. The remaining $140,000 would have been gravy—free money to be used as they wished (though I would hope they would invest it for their future).

If property values continued to rise (which they've been doing in Calgary at a good clip) and their new house eventually came to be worth $440,000, they could then sell it and take another $200,000 in tax-free profits.

In the kind of bull market we saw in real estate during the first five years of the twenty-first century, countless home-owners used this approach to build wealth tax-free. It requires you to stay on top of the real estate market in your area and move more frequently, but it can and does work. Of course, if and when real estate markets cool down, this strategy will take much longer to achieve results. But given the long-term upwards trend in real estate values, its ultimate success is usually a matter of when, not if.

STRATEGY NO. 4:
BUY UP TO THE
NEXT NEIGHBOURHOOD

This is probably the most common approach to real estate investing. You buy a home, live it in for a while, grow your family—and your income—and then eventually move to a bigger home in a better neighbourhood.

This ultimately creates leverage for you because you are now living in a more expensive home, and as it appreciates in value, your equity grows faster. (After all, while a 6 percent increase in the value of a $100,000 home will add $6,000 to its owner's equity, the same rise in the value of a $1 million home will make its owner $60,000 richer.)

I'm a classic example of this. Even though I procrastinated in the beginning, I eventually went from my first house—a $220,000 fixer-upper in the suburbs—to a $640,000 condo in San Francisco to a $2 million loft in New York that, as of this writing, is easily worth $3 million. The market could drop, of course, but at this point chances are that the loft is always going to be worth more than we paid for it.

The point is that, at each step, the profits I made from the appreciation of my old home allowed me to buy a much more expensive new home. In this way, even without getting into the rental game, I've been able to buy three homes over the last fifteen years—and in the process, increase my net worth by well over $1 million.

At this point, we could sell our loft and leverage up yet again. We just looked at a penthouse in a new development that would cost us $3.5 million. It's slightly smaller than our current place, but the building is new and "hot." My guess is that this new property has more upside than our current home. Probably a lot more upside.

So should we take another ride on the leverage express? It's what a lot of people do.

In the end, it's a personal decision. What you need to consider with this approach is that as you leverage up, your life becomes more expensive and often more complicated. Your apartment is more expensive, your neighbourhood is more expensive, and your overhead just keeps getting bigger.

THINK ABOUT WHAT
THE MARTINS DID

I'm not sharing any of this to brag. I'm sharing it to show you how simple homeownership simply builds tremendous wealth. It took me a decade of hard work to save $1 million.

It took me thirty-six months to increase my net worth by another $1 million by simply being a homeowner in a hot market. We could have been renting a loft in New York this whole time and not made a cent. I'd say half of my friends in New York are doing just that. They thought we were crazy to buy in 2002—because the real estate market in New York supposedly couldn't get any hotter than it was then.

If you go back to the Martins for a second, remember that they also traded up three times. They went from a $30,000 home to a $100,000 home to a $650,000 home. When they sold that last house, it was worth $2 million. Then they stopped—and downsized to the right size. They bought a new, smaller home in a less-expensive area in Arizona. And they used some of their profits to buy a four-plex rental from which they now earn $90,000 a year in positive cash flow.

IT MAY SOUND TOO EASY TO BE TRUE, BUT IT REALLY DOES WORK

As you read this, the strategies I'm discussing and the stories I'm telling may seem too simple. If it's that easy, why isn't everyone rich? But keep one thing in mind. None of this stuff just happens. You have to take action.

The Martins didn't just happen to acquire their multi-million-dollar net worth. They didn't just accidentally become Automatic Millionaire Homeowners. They made a series of decisions at various points in their life that at times were scary. Their first home purchase, for only $30,000, was scary. They really didn't think they could afford it. Their rent was low, the neighbourhood where they could afford to buy was not ideal, and they could have easily just kept renting. But they went for it.

When they decided to rent out their first home, they were scared. They didn't know if they would like being landlords. It wasn't all easy. Not all their tenants were perfect. They toughed it out, however, and never got rid of that first property.

They also were scared when they bought bigger and more expensive homes. Buying that $750,000 dream home of theirs was a huge decision. They never thought that it would go up in value the way it did. And there were plenty of times they thought they had over-extended themselves.

I can relate. When we bought our Tribeca loft I was plenty nervous. Ask my wife, Michelle. We were the first people to buy in our building—on the first day. Half the condos sold in a week. Then the New York real estate market started to slow. For six months, it literally just froze. Every week, the developer of my building would reduce his prices. The last condos to sell went for as much as $250,000 below their original price. By the end of those six months, the loft we had bought for $2,000,000 was probably worth $500,000 less than what we'd paid for it. If we had to sell it then, we could have lost all our equity.

But we stayed put. The Martins stayed put. Things worked out. They often do.

As the Martins' dream home soared in value from $750,000 to $2 million, they decided to continue their journey. They looked at retirement communities where living costs were cheaper. They investigated Arizona. Many of their friends thought they were crazy. "Move to the desert?" they said. "What are you thinking?"

What they were thinking was that they wanted to retire, and to do that they needed to reduce their overhead. "Let's use our real estate profits," they said to each other, "and retire early."

Which is what they did. But they were scared when they did it. They didn't know they would like Arizona (which is why they rented there for a year before buying).

And they were scared to buy a four-plex as an investment property.

But it all worked out.

NOTHING GREAT IS EVER EASY—AND IT'S ALMOST ALWAYS SCARY

My point is this: nothing I've shared with you in this book is risk free. The same can be said of my experience. It may be simple, but it's not easy.

Let me say that again. *Getting rich through homeownership may be simple, but it's not always easy.* You can take this chapter and read it ten times. Not one of these ideas will ever be a "no-brainer" for you. You will have to stretch your comfort level if you're going to do anything more than simply buy a house and live it in for the rest of your life.

Of course, if that's all you do—just buy a house, pay it down early, and live in it for the rest of your while its value appreciates—**that's still a lot better than renting for the rest of your life and making someone else rich!**

AUTOMATIC MILLIONAIRE HOMEOWNER ACTION STEPS

Reviewing the actions we laid out in this chapter, here's what you should be doing right now to go from being an ordinary homeowner to an Automatic Millionaire Homeowner.

❑ Reread the story of John and Lucy Martin in Chapter One and start thinking of your home not simply as a place to live but as a vehicle for building wealth.

❑ Check to see if rents in your area for a house like yours are high enough for you to consider becoming a landlord.

❑ Calculate how much equity you have in your house and consider a cash-out refinancing, a series of sales with tax-free profits, or "leveraging up."

❑ Above all, commit to taking action.

CHAPTER ELEVEN

HOW TO "BUBBLE-PROOF" YOUR REAL ESTATE PLAN— AND SURVIVE A DOWNTURN

For the previous ten chapters, I've been encouraging you to go out and buy a home because it will ultimately be the best investment you ever make. So why switch the focus now to the downside of real estate? Well, the fact is that real estate has cycles. Just like the stock market, real estate prices don't always go up. The fact is, they can go down.

I've been around the business long enough to remember the real estate boom of the early 1980s, and I remember the California real estate crash that followed it in the late 1980s. My first job after I graduated from the University of Southern California in 1990 was as a commercial real estate agent in Pleasanton, California, where I had the privilege of working on some of the largest corporate accounts in northern California (including companies like Pacific Bell, AT&T, and Prudential). From 1990 to 1993, I worked on tens of millions of dollars worth of leases and commercial sales. I remember doing a search for 500,000 square feet of office space for one of our clients. We wound up touring more than fifteen buildings in the Bay Area—all of them empty!

"What happened here?" I asked my boss. "How can there be so many buildings of this size sitting around empty?"

"It's called a down cycle," he replied. "It happens every twenty years. Developers overbuild, banks overlend, people get overexcited and overextend. They all think the good times will go on forever, but they don't."

He was right. Inevitably, any boom will bust. It happens over and over again, but no one ever seems to learn.

THE RESIDENTIAL MARKET WASN'T ANY BETTER

If you had bought a home at the peak of the California real estate market in the late 1980s, it would be nearly a decade before your house would once again be worth what you probably paid for it. As a result, many, many people who for one reason or another had to sell their houses during this period were forced into bankruptcy because they couldn't get the price they had paid. They ended up owing more than their properties were worth—and often had no choice but simply to give their houses back to the bank. Canadian homeowners in cities like Toronto and Vancouver faced a similar predicament. Some of them simply dropped the keys to their houses on the kitchen counter and walked away.

As I write this in July 2005, after thirteen straight years of steady—and, in some cases, startling—increases in home prices, cracks are beginning to show in the real estate market. There are signs—at least in certain parts of the U.S. and Canada—that things may be cooling off.

It's getting scary. With some experts predicting a real estate meltdown, you need to protect yourself.

Here's how you can do that.

FIVE SIMPLE WAYS TO PROTECT YOURSELF FROM A REAL ESTATE MELTDOWN

1. MAKE SURE YOU CAN AFFORD YOUR MORTGAGE

This book is primarily about building wealth through home-ownership. That means owning the house you live in or rent out. Not the house you buy just to flip. The buy-and-flip book is someone else's. What we're talking about here is the common-sense approach to building your wealth through homeownership.

What does that mean? Well, to begin with, it means not buying a house you can't really afford.

You may not be able to afford your home, if . . .

• You put nothing down.
• You don't have a savings "cushion" big enough to cover several months' worth of mortgage payments.

I'm not saying you shouldn't buy a home if either of these things apply to you. As we saw in John and Lucy Martin's story, there's nothing wrong with stretching a little in order to become a homeowner. It certainly beats continuing to rent. BUT you should still be sensible, which means regarding those signs I just listed as "red flags." If either of them applies to you, it means you are taking a risk when you buy a home in a booming real estate market.

According to Statistics Canada, household debt has grown more quickly than income over the last decade. But net worth—the total value of a person's assets, including house, car, etc.—rose even more quickly. This is because the value of people's houses has gone up considerably over the last few years. As long as this continues, and as long as Canadian homeowner have enough income to pay their debts, then they have nothing to worry about. But when real estate values go down, the problems might begin, especially for people who bought a bigger house than they could afford.

When interest rates skyrocket and home prices drop—both of which are very real possibilities—you end up with a "double whammy." People who bought homes they couldn't really afford are suddenly in trouble because their mortgage payments are jumping by 10 percent to 20 percent. But they can't sell because, with prices dropping, their homes are now worth less than they owe on them.

This stuff happens. In fact, it happens almost predictably—coming around just like a comet about every twenty years.

So what should you do?

BUBBLE-PROOF YOUR PROPERTY

Here are five ways you can protect yourself.

- Lock in your mortgage interest rate—ideally, by getting a five-year or seven-year fixed-rate mortgage. (Some lenders even offer ten-year terms.)
- If you have a variable-rate mortgage, refinance while rates are still low and lock in the rate for at least five years. The longer the better. Even if you're planning to sell in less than five years, lock in your rate for a longer period to protect yourself in case you run into a down cycle during which selling may not make sense.
- Pay a little extra on your mortgage every month so that your principal balance shrinks as quickly as possible.
- Don't borrow equity out of your house to cover living expenses, take trips, pay off credit cards, buy a car, etc. Home equity should be used only to purchase more real estate or to improve your house in ways that will increase its value (such as adding a bathroom or deck, or renovating a kitchen).
- Start building an emergency savings account; aim to have six months' worth of housing costs in the bank—and Make It Automatic!

2. THINK LOCAL

At the end of the day, the only real estate market that should matter to you is the one you are in! Real estate is talked about a lot nationally—as in "the national average home price went up over 10 percent in the last year." **What the market does nationally is irrelevant to you.** In fact, what the market does on the other side of town doesn't always matter to you. What you care about is the value of your house or condo, which literally can depend on which street you live on or which building you live in. If your home is in Regina, Saskatchewan, what's happening in the Vancouver condo market is pretty much meaningless, unless you happen also to own a condo in Vancouver.

Here's how to keep on top of *your* real estate market:

READ ABOUT AND DRIVE THE MARKET

Open the local newspaper and look at the real estate section. Are there homes like yours for sale? Are there a lot of them? Check out the paper every week. Does it look like the same homes are for sale week after week, month after month? Are they moving or not? Next, drive around your neighbourhood looking for "For Sale" signs. Are they everywhere—or are there only a few? Again, does it look like homes are selling?

VISIT OPEN HOUSES

The best way to get a quick feel for the pulse of your market is to visit open houses on the weekend. Are they packed with people looking to buy? Ask the real estate agents hosting the open houses, "How's the market?" After you've spoken to a half dozen of them over the course of a single Saturday afternoon, you should have a pretty good sense of what's going on in your area.

If the market is tight and houses are selling, you can relax. If not, you should prepare for a down cycle—meaning you should take care not to overextend yourself, watch your expenses carefully, and try your best to avoid a situation where you may be forced to sell.

3. GET THE FACTS

When you own (or are thinking of buying) an investment property, there are a handful of really important things you should know about your market: what the housing inventory is like, where prices are going, and how long homes are sitting on the market. The fastest way to get this information is to meet with a great real estate agent who specializes in your neighbourhood. Here are some key questions to ask that agent to find out what's happening in your local marketplace.

Inventory: How many homes like yours are for sale in the area? The key phrase here is "homes like yours." It doesn't matter if there are fifty homes for sale in your neighbourhood if only five are like yours. You need to compare what's in the market that's the same size, age, quality, and style as your home with the total number of homes for sale. If an appreciable fraction (say, more than 15 percent or 20 percent) is very similar to your home, you may face a challenge getting top dollar.

Prices: What are homes like yours selling for? Earlier, we discussed the importance of getting the "comps." If you're thinking about selling in the near future, ask your real estate agent to give you monthly updates on sale prices of comparable homes.

Time on the market: When a home goes on the market, the selling agent tracks how many days it takes to find a buyer. These numbers are looked at both nationally and locally as a key indicator of whether a market is heating up or cooling down. Obviously, the longer it takes to sell a home, the cooler the market is. Of course, this is just one indicator, and it often gets skewed by anomalies—a home that sells in a day or one that sits unsold for a year. Still, you want to know what's happening in your area. Are homes moving fast or moving slower?

4. DON'T BUY A HOUSE OR CONDO JUST TO "FLIP" IT

This book is about investing—about buying a home and using it as the foundation of your financial security. If you buy a rental property, it has to be capable of generating positive cash flow. If that's not a reasonable expectation, then you shouldn't buy it. And even if you're confident a property will fetch a high enough rent to cover the costs, you still shouldn't buy it if you don't have at least three months' worth of mortgage payments in the bank—just in case it takes you a while to find a tenant.

Most important of all, don't go out in a hot market and buy a new condo in a new building that's not yet built in the hope that you will be able flip it for a quick and easy profit. You may buy a flip and end up flopping—particularly if you buy in a booming market with new condo towers going up on every block. A few months or years down the road, when the market is flooded with these new condos, and everyone else is hoping to flip theirs, you could easily find yourself with a real challenge. And don't assume that, if you can't sell, you'll be able to just rent it out. The rental market falls, too. When there are more condos going up than there are people buying, rents will decline. More likely, you'll find yourself stuck with mortgage payments you can't afford. So think seriously about this before you just leap in.

With any investment, the best time to leap into a hot market may be after it's cooled and others are scrambling to sell.

5. KNOW THAT, IN MOST CASES, TIME CURES ALL

The one great certainty with real estate is that, over the long term, time cures all ... at least in most cases. What this means is that areas that go bust eventually come back. Every great city has had its bleak periods, but invariably they recover from them.

New York City in the 1970s was brutal. Then it boomed in the early 1980s. And then it went bust again. By the early

1990s, you couldn't give away a condo there. I remember a friend of mine who bought a brand new, three-bedroom condo on the upper East Side back then for $180,000. Her dad lent her the down payment and said, "Get some friends to rent the other two bedrooms. In a decade, you'll be rich."

We all thought he was crazy. Well, today that condo is worth well over $2 million. New York City real estate came back with a vengeance. The same is true of markets all over Canada, from Vancouver to Calgary to Toronto. Markets boom, then go bust, then boom again.

In the end, what matters is whether you have the resources to ride out the cycle. If your time frame is short and you buy near the end of an up cycle, there's a good chance you're going to get hurt. But if you can hang on for the long haul—say, at least seven years, which is the average length of time Canadians own their homes—you shouldn't have anything to worry about, even if the bubble in your area pops.

Remember—being an Automatic Homeowner Millionaire isn't about timing the market. **It's about time in the market. It's when you're *not* trying to get rich quick that you get rich slowly.**

AUTOMATIC MILLIONAIRE HOMEOWNER ACTION STEPS

Reviewing the actions we laid out in this chapter, here's what you should be doing right now to "bubble-proof" your real estate plan.

❑ Make sure you can afford your mortgage.

❑ Find out what's selling and for how much in your neighbourhood.

❑ Don't try to make a "quick killing." Think long-term.

❑ Make sure you have the resources to ride out the real estate cycle.

CHAPTER TWELVE

MAKE A DIFFERENCE— HELP SOMEONE ELSE BECOME A HOMEOWNER

We've spent the last few hours looking at how you can build a foundation for real wealth through homeownership. Becoming an *Automatic Millionaire Homeowner* is now truly within your reach. Indeed, I hope you've already begun your journey. If not, I hope that, when you put this book down, you'll be inspired to start making it happen. But before we end our time together, I want to share one more idea—one additional thing you can do to change your life for the better.

HAPPINESS BEGINS WITH GIVING

Many people read my books and become inspired to make their lives richer and more secure. That's certainly my goal, but I also want to inspire my readers to help others. When I wrote *The Automatic Millionaire* (the book that led to this one), I ended it with a chapter called "Give Back Automatically." This chapter was about the importance of helping others and the power of making that kind of giving automatic. It shared the message of how giving back to others a piece of what we bring in for ourselves can make the world a better place.

This is something I believe with all my heart. The fact is, there is more to life than money. Now this may strike you as a strange thing to read in a book about how to become a millionaire through homeownership. But it's true. In fact, not only is it true, it is also important.

Now don't get me wrong. Money is good, and I sincerely hope you get the riches you want. But money will not give your life meaning.

What will is giving something back. As I see it, the only reason to learn how to make more money and build wealth is ultimately to be able to help others. We are put here to make the world a better place. And here's something amazing. Although you should give simply for the sake of giving, the reality is that abundance tends to flow back to those who give. *The more you give, the more comes back to you. It is the flow of abundance that brings us more joy, more love, more wealth, and more meaning in our lives.*

After *The Automatic Millionaire* was published, countless readers wrote to tell me that this final chapter was what ultimately inspired them to become Automatic Millionaires—that what got them motivated was not simply the idea of having more but the idea of being able to give more.

I share this story because I want to end this book in a similar way—by teaching you how you can give something back as an Automatic Millionaire Homeowner. After you've become a homeowner (or, indeed, while you're in the process of doing it), there is an extremely practical and effective way you can help others do the same—and I'd like to make sure you know about it.

A GREAT WAY TO HELP OTHERS GET A HOME AND BUILD A FUTURE

If, after having read this book, you believe as I do that the best route to personal financial security is through homeownership, then you should also believe that one of the best ways to end poverty would be to find a way to put even those who can't afford it into their own homes. CMHC puts the number of Canadian households unable to find decent housing they can afford at about 15 percent, although this percentage has been falling in recent years. While most Canadians live in housing that's affordable, uncrowded and in a good state of repair, says a CMHC report, the need for housing remains high among seniors aged sixty-five or over living alone, lone parents with children under eighteen living at home, recent immigrants, and Aboriginal households.

Helping all these people find homes may seem like an impossible goal, but it's not. In fact, there are numerous charitable organizations doing just this every day.

HOW YOU CAN HELP

If the idea of helping someone else get into a home appeals to you, there are literally hundreds of organizations to which you can contribute both time and money. I've listed three really worthy ones below, but they are just the tip of the iceberg. Do some research of your own through websites like Canadian Donors Guide (**www.donorsguide.ca**) or Volunteer.ca (**www.volunteer.ca**), and find a group in your own community that could use your help.

Habitat for Humanity Canada
40 Albert St.
Waterloo, ON N2L 3S2
www.habitat.ca
1-800-667-5137

Since 1976, Habitat for Humanity has helped build more than 200,000 homes in upwards of 100 countries around the world—sheltering more than 1 million people in some 3,000 communities worldwide. The basic philosophy isn't to give homes away to anyone, but to give poor people who are willing to work hard a chance to earn the homes they need and deserve. In Canada, Habitat for Humanity builds or renovates homes, then helps low-income families (generally those with incomes 30 percent to 50 percent below the median for their area) buy them with no-interest loans and down payments as modest as $500. But need alone is not enough to qualify for a Habitat house—the family must also contribute substantial "sweat equity," typically putting in 300 to 500 hours helping to build or renovate their home or someone else's. As a volunteer, you literally raise the frames and pound the nails to help make it possible for a family to one day sleep under their own roof.

Charity Village
www.charityvillage.com.

This website bills itself as "Canada's supersite for the non-profit sector." With a few minutes of your time, you can track down housing-related initiatives in your community, listed under a heading such as "Community services" or "Housing" in each province.

Raising the Roof
200–263 Eglinton Ave. West
Toronto (ON)
M4R 1B1
www.raisingtheroof.org
416-481-1838

Raising the Roof is Canada's only national charity dedicated to long-term solutions to homelessness. The organization builds awareness about homelessness and what can be done and raises funds for community groups working to alleviate homelessness.

NOW MAKE IT AUTOMATIC

If you decide to contribute your sweat equity by volunteering for an organization like Habitat for Humanity or Raising the Roof, more power to you. But if you decide to make a financial contribution to one of the charities listed on the websites here, make up your mind to Make It Automatic. Many charities encourage people to become regular supporters by contributing a small amount monthly, using an automatic funds transfer.

Homeownership lets you get rich where you sleep. Automatic giving lets you help others while you sleep.

WHAT I'M DOING TO HELP OTHERS

Because I think it is so important that we help others become financially secure through homeownership, I'm marking the publication of this book with a $50,000 donation from my FinishRich Foundation to Habitat for Humanity. Habitat will also be getting a portion of the royalties from every copy of this book sold in the United States and Canada in 2006. So if you're thinking about buying a copy of this book for a friend, keep in mind that a portion of the sales price will be going to help a needy family get a home of their own.

JOIN THE GREAT CANADIAN HOMEOWNER CHALLENGE™

The publication of this book is really just the beginning of my mission to help tenants become homeowners. I believe so strongly that the secret to financial independence and security is homeownership that I will be touring Canada after the publication of this book, hosting FREE educational events as part of what we're calling *The Great Canadian Homeowner Challenge*. This initiative will be focused on helping anyone who wants to buy a home get into a home. Specifically, we are working to inspire 10 million people in North America to buy homes over the next ten years.

I hope this book has inspired you—and that you will join us at an event. Visit our website (**www.finishrich.com**) for details on when I'll be in your area.

TELL A FRIEND—SHARE THE DREAM!

I hope you close this book inspired to make homeownership your path to financial freedom. Nothing helps you achieve success faster than helping others. So please consider sharing what you've learned in this book with someone you love—particularly if they are still a tenant. Lend this book to them. Suggest they take it out from the library. Pass along some of the e-mail links to my free audios on homeownership.

If you want to buy a copy of this book for a friend, that's great—but please know that my goal isn't simply to sell more books. It's to share the message. And the best way I know to do that is for you to live what you learn and prove it works.

Together, we can really make a difference.

YOUR
JOURNEY HOME
BEGINS TODAY!

I want you to know that I am proud of you for coming so far in this journey. You bought this book—and you read it! Well done. Now go use what you've learned to make your life the way you want and the world the way it can be.

This book was written to be a simple guide filled with simple ideas about how you can become an Automatic Millionaire Homeowner. I've tried to make it as powerful and action oriented as possible, to arm you with ideas, strategies, and action steps designed to get you going on the road to wealth and financial security through homeownership.

But you must "get going." And you should do it today.

The one thing I know for sure is that, over the long term, real estate prices are going up. Maybe not tomorrow or next year—but long term, they are going up. They always have.

Even if the real estate markets cool, I promise that twenty years from now you'll look back and think, "Wow, I can't believe how cheap that property was twenty years ago!"

Remember—**as long as you're alive, you have to live somewhere.** So does everyone else you know. And because of that, homeownership will continue to be a great investment.

SO NOW IT'S UP TO YOU

You are an amazing person. Deep down inside, you know you can do this. So go do it.

Don't let the markets, the difficulties, or the skeptics keep you from going for your dreams.

If you are renting and want to own a home—go make it happen.

If you own a home and want to own a bigger home—go make it happen.

If you want to own rental properties—go make it happen.

And if you want to give back—**GO MAKE IT HAPPEN!**

Your life is short. Live it to its fullest. *Live it rich.*

BE INSPIRED!

AUTOMATIC MILLIONAIRE
HOMEOWNER SUCCESS STORIES

When *The Automatic Millionaire Homeowner* was first published in 2006, I partnered with Wells Fargo Home Mortgage to launch The Great American Homeowner Challenge™. Over the last year and a half, we've worked together toward fulfilling our mission of inspiring and empowering 10 million people to build lifelong financial security through homeownership.

As part of The Great American Homeowner Challenge, we held an essay contest and received more than twenty-one thousand personal stories about homeownership from people all across the country. To those who participated, we thank you for your amazing submissions. We are touched and honored to be part of your personal journey toward homeownership.

More than ninety monthly winners of our Take the Challenge(tm) essay contest were chosen, and each received $2,500 toward their monthly mortgage payment. And our grand prize winner, Vicente Adame, was awarded $250,000 (after taxes) toward the purchase of a home! Vicente's winning essay appears below, followed by additional essays and reader success stories. It's stories like these that inspire me to do what I do, and I hope they inspire you to take action in your own life as well. I would love to include *your* story in a future book. To share your story, log on to www.finishrich.com.

When I was a child, I was a dreamer and fully determined to make something of my life, but I could not have imagined the dream my life would become—a dream that began when I made the decision to buy my first home. You see, I was born thirty-four years ago in a one-room dirt-floor house in a rural village of Mexico. Without plumbing or electricity, we bathed, cleaned clothes, and washed dishes in a small creek nearby.

At sixteen, I was brought to live with family in the United States, where I attended school and learned English. Although I worked very hard and excelled in my job, I had very little to show for my money.

I took a life-turning step that set my dreams in motion when I bought a simple bungalow. At the time, it didn't seem like a major decision; I simply didn't want to pay rent any longer. However, the freedom I felt was something I wanted to share with the world. As equity built up, I used it to buy a home for my mother, and another for my brother the year after that. This was amazing! I then purchased a commercial property. With the rents received, I've invested in four additional properties.

Five years after purchasing my first small home, I moved to a beautiful, four-bedroom Victorian on a street straight out of a story book.

Last year, I became a Realtor—the only Spanish-speaking Realtor in our area—because I enjoy nothing more than helping others find the life-changing freedom in owning their own homes. I try to imagine going back in time to tell the seven-year-old at work in the fields that some day he would own a big beautiful dream home, and that his children would go to school and play without ever worrying about their family's finances. That determined little boy would have laughed at the fairy tale I was telling him. Then, he would have gone back to work to make that dream come true.

—VICENTE ADAME

It was January 2004, and I had been living in New York City for two years. I was thrity-one and making just under $50,000 a year. My only account was a checking account, and my monthly bank statement read close to $5,000 remaining. I was living from paycheque to paycheque. My financial outlook was grim and, for the first time in my life, I started to think about what that meant. I was finally starting to grow up and realizing I didn't want to live like a college kid forever. I wanted things—nice things—and, more important, I wanted a secure financial future.

One day around this time, I was watching Oprah when David was a guest on the show. He was talking about his book, The Automatic Millionaire. The things he was saying made sense to me. There were simple changes people could make that could change their lives. I remember writing down David's name and the name of the book on a piece of paper and sticking in my wallet. Shortly thereafter, I purchased the book and literally read it from cover to cover without putting it down. Although all his points made sense, the section that was the most poignant to me was the one about the vitality of owning your home.

Living in New York, I never thought I could afford to buy a home. Nobody owns in New York. You have to be really rich to buy something in New York. This was the common perception, as well as my own. But as I began investigating, I realized that I could afford to buy something! Okay, maybe it wouldn't be huge, and maybe it wouldn't be exactly the neighborhood that would be my first choice, but there were properties—in nice areas—that I could afford. I could own my first home!

I had narrowed my search to a few neighborhoods that I liked and could afford. I had decided I could go up to around $150,000. Even that was a stretch, but I thought if I scrimped a bit I could pull it off. I had also spoken to several mortgage companies and they had agreed that based on my financial situation, this was my upper limit. Since I had only $5000 in cash, I was going to have to take money out of my 401K and borrow a little money from my parents to come up with the down payment and closing costs.

One of the neighborhoods I was considering was Hoboken, New Jersey. Hoboken is a small city directly across the Hudson River from Manhattan. It's is a great place with a cozy college-town feel and, most important, a super-easy commute to Manhattan—only one stop on the PATH train! Unfortunately, I wasn't finding anything for less than $200,000, and I was about to give up hope. Then I saw a listing for a 300 square-foot studio condominium for $160,000. I knew instantly that it was a great deal. I made an offer on the spot and ultimately bought it for $154,000. I was a homeowner!

Six months after I bought the condo, a similar unit next door went up for sale for $180,000. After a bidding war, the unit sold within two weeks for $185,000. I contacted the realtor who sold it to ask how much he thought I could get for mine. Based on some of the features of my condo and the renovations I had made, I knew that my unit was a little nicer. Sure enough, he said $200,000. My mind was racing. I had made $46,000 in six months! I began to think about selling and taking the earnings to buy a place in Manhattan (where I ultimately wanted to live).

Before I could blink, my condo was on the market for $205,000. The unit had been listed for less than forty-eight hours when I received an offer of $200,000. Initially I was extremely excited, but then I remembered what David says in his book about holding on to properties when you move. If you can rent it for enough to cover your expenses, why would you sell? When you rent, your property continues to appreciate as your tenant pays down your mortgage—not to mention the tax write-off you get from the interest on your mortgage. David states that "homeowners get rich, but landlords get really rich." I can tell you from experience that this is absolutely true. In the case of my Hoboken condo, I could not only cover my mortgage, taxes, and maintenance with the rent I got, but I could actually pocket $200 over and above my expenses. So ultimately, that's what I did!

Before doing so, I began to look for properties in Manhattan. I finally found a condominium on Twenty-third Street in Chelsea. It wasn't exactly where I wanted to be in the city, but it was in Manhattan! The building was being converted from rentals to condos and the process was not yet complete. They were asking for $250,000 for the unit I wanted. We settled on $240,000. That meant I needed to come up with $24,000 for the down payment and an additional $5,000 for closing costs. As this unit would not be ready to close until the conversion was done, I didn't end up closing on the property until almost a year *after I signed the contract. During this time, I lived in the Hoboken condo. By the time the closing for the Twenty-third Street condo arrived, the Hoboken condo was worth approximately $225,000. My mortgage now was around $135,000, and I had about $90,000 in equity. So I took out a home equity loan to cover my down payment and closing costs on the Twenty-third Street unit. I closed on the new property in June 2005. From the time I signed the sales contract in September 2004 to the time I closed in June 2005, the offering price in the building, for my same exact unit, had gone up to $300,000. The unit had appreciated by $60,000 before I had even closed on it. I was now the owner of two properties—and I was a landlord.*

In January 2006, I decided to do it again. I bought, this time with my partner, an eight-hundred square-foot, one-bedroom cooperative on the Upper West Side for $550,000. The building is directly across from Riverside Park, and it's beautiful. Again, I used the equity from the Twenty-third Street unit to cover the down payment and closing costs. The rent I am getting from the two-rental unit covers all my expenses on the units and leaves me a little extra to contribute to my current mortgage. As real estate is always volatile, it is hard to know exactly how much equity there is between the three properties. But based on current market values in July 2007, minus all mortgages, it's probably somewhere between $400,000 and $500,000.

July 2007, I started looking for number four. To be continued . . .

—MARK RUGGIERO

(Note: Mark's story was featured on ABC's 20/20)

I boarded the plane to America on my forthieth birthday with $400 in my pocket. My name is Dorulet Moga. I am from a small village in Romania. I faced many challenges in my journey to homeownership. I could not speak English, nor did I have status as a citizen of the United States.

My life changed the second I met my beautiful wife. After our marriage, I obtained my green card and began working double shifts as a security guard. I cleaned houses on weekends for extra money, and saved every dollar in order to put my dreams into action. My dream was simple: to save enough money for a down payment on a house. I wanted to give my wife a beautiful home, start a family, and begin a new life.

I knew America was the place where dreams come true if you work hard. Every person is equal in this country, and opportunity is everywhere. I love America!

I spent every Sunday for several months going to open houses and speaking with listing agents. I found our dream house on February 22, 2002. I asked many questions and learned the meanings of many new words, new words such as: fico score, amortization, escrow, and non-contingent offer. I felt like I learned a whole new English. I had never written an offer in my life, but the agent told me the market was very "hot" in southern California so I wrote the offer for asking price on that day.

Since that day, my wife and I have raised two beautiful children in that home. We were able to purchase two additional homes with the increased equity we cashed out of our first home. We still own our first home, and soon tenants will pay the mortgage on it.

Anyone who says homeownership is impossible or that challenges are too great to overcome should listen to my story. I am living proof that dreams come true. I was an immigrant with no money who could not speak English. If I can make it here, anyone can.

—DORULET MOGA

Last Christmas I was in Puerto Vallarta celebrating my parents' fiftieth wedding anniversary and I brought The Automatic Millionaire Homeowner with me to read on the beach. By the time I got through it I had declared 2006 to be "the year of real estate." I had been talking about getting a rental property for years but I needed a push. Well, on December first, we purchased a great second house in a town up the coast, which we rent out.

Your book empowered us to take charge of our financial life by making some important changes. We increased our automatic retirement savings from 12% to 18%, and had our life insurance policy updated and our disability coverage reviewed. We also made the difficult decision to get a new financial advisor. I look forward to learning more and taking more active steps to improve our life. Thanks so very much.

—CAROLYN BENTLEY

David,
I attended your Automatic Millionaire Homeowner event at the Jacob Javits Center in New York, New York on March 9, 2006. I

found your words to be very motivating. I received a copy of your book at that event and read it shortly afterward. I look forward to reading your other titles. We need more people like you to share the wealth of information.

Well, the year has not yet ended and I am now a homeowner. My other half and I decided to look outside of our box. We did our research and found that Binghamton, New York offers very affordable housing. It is within our range and we found a 2010 square foot, four-bedroom, two bath home that we like. We are so happy.

Best wishes,

—ABIGAIL RYAN

About eight months ago my sister Darlene came to me with The Automatic Millionaire. *She told me she had read the book, loved it, and recommended it to me. At that time my wife and I were renting one side of a two-family home from my parents. Darlene was renting the other side with her husband, Don, and their son, DJ. The rent was very cheap for both of us—thanks to our generous parents. At the time I started reading* The Automatic Millionaire, *I was twenty-six years old, married for two years, in debt and with little savings. By the time I finished the book I had set up an IRA account and was automatically depositing $200.00 a month and my wife was maxing out her 401K plan at work. We opened a high interest saving account with ING Direct, and were able to cut our debt almost in half.*

Inspired and determined, I purchased David's latest book, The Automatic Millionaire Homeowner. *My sister also bought* *the book. One month after reading it, my sister purchased her first home. When I heard the news, I also took David's advice and approached my parents about selling me the two-family house I was renting from them. They agreed to sell the house to me for $508,000. I found a loan, got approved, and purchased the home. The house was appraised at $635,000. I still live in the smaller unit of the house and rent the larger side for $1700 a month. I would just like to thank David for getting me off my butt and helping me start thinking about my future and tackling it full on.*

—DAVE MULIK

I attended your homeowner workshop in Seattle, Washington last year, and I am now about to purchase my first home! I close on April 19 on a two- bedroom condo with a view of the sound. I would not have been able to do it without your book, The Automatic Millionaire Homeowner. *I read each chapter and I gave myself a week to complete the checklists at the end of every chapter—my homework.*

I created an automatic plan to pay off all my credit card debt and opened an automatic savings account with ING Direct for my house (thanks for the suggestion!). I also started a game with the Latte Factor. Every time I wanted to buy a latte in the coffee shop downstairs from my office I would walk across the street from my office building to the bank and deposit the money in my house account. I also had a garage sale and put all the money I made into my house account. I then deposited my tax return into my house account!

Before I knew it, I had $1,000, then $2,000 and then $3,000. I found a great loan officer and real estate agent and attended a couple of workshops for condo- and home-buyers in my area. I also checked the programs offered by my credit union and the State Department of Housing and I found a great loan! I got so into this that my friends started to ask me for advice, and now a couple of them already have enough to cover their closing costs! Anyway, I found a place, made and offer, and, oh boy! This has been the most stressful thing I have ever done! I am stretching myself, but I figure that a year of not going out to dinner every night, bringing my lunches to work, and not taking trips here and there every month are worth letting go of for a future of financial security. Your workshop made such an impact in my life that I am even thinking of becoming a loan officer so I can help others to start their path to wealth. Thank you so much!

—JACQUE LARRAINZAR

David, Thank you is all I can say (and not nearly enough). The Automatic Millionaire *changed my life. Here is my story: I am proudly serving in the United States Navy on active duty. Before I read your book, I was six years into my career, and approaching thirty. I was still paying rent but had a head start on the average American because I had no credit card debt and a couple thousand dollars in savings. I was, however, still technically living from paycheque to paycheque. I had no plan for retirement. Well, I read* The Automatic Millionaire, *put its ideals into practice, and now five years later, I bought a house that* *made me 90,000 right off the bat, and I have also saved approximately $50,000 in cash and retirement assets through various investment vehicles.*

Taking your advice on paying down principal early, I set my payments up automatically and submit two extra full house payments per year. At this rate, my home will be paid off in twelve years versus thirty and I will have saved tens of thousands in interest, not to mention that the house (now a rental property) is bringing in positive cash flow. I will be financially comfortable by age forty-three, with all the leisure time in the world to enjoy life and pursue other business and investment opportunities. I estimate I should have $250,000 to $300,000 in cash and investment assets, and I will own at least one house outright. I will have a pension and NO mortgage! Thanks again.

—STG1 Marc Boucher, USN

Dear David, I'm like the children's choo-choo train. I never knew that I could . . . until I met you here at the Baltimore Convention Center with your book The Automatic Millionaire Homeowner. Since then we bought our vacation condo in Ocean City, and we took advantage of our 401(k) and 403(b). plans. We came to this great country in 1989 with just two suitcases. I wish we could have met you then. I know we would have been millionaires by now. We made lots of mistakes but now we are living the American Dream: a home with a two-car garage, two kids, one dog, and a condo for vacation. Thanks to you we also have a will, a retirement basket, saving basket, and a security basket. Now my goal is to get rid of our credit card debt.

   Thanks again,

—SILVIA AND PETER PETRIK

My husband and I met in 1997, married two years later in September, 1999, and formed a combined family of three children who were three, four and five at the time we met. We always knew that we needed to buy a home and start building equity. We saw what our family members were doing and wanted to do the same. In 2002 my husband spotted a small sign posted by a local builder on a telephone pole in Yuba City. It read: 1st phase now released. He called me and asked, "Are you ready to move?" The rest is history!

   We put $11,000 down on a $175,000 loan and purchased a four-bedroom, 1,700 square foot home on a tiny lot. That was January 2003. Our dream was to own a home on five acres, so after building up our equity, we took a home equity loan for the 20% down payment on a nice piece of property. We were nervous, but we kept telling ourselves that the long-term results would pay off. We soon sold our first home, purchased a camping trailer, secured a construction loan to build and moved the three kids, two dogs, and our cat, onto a vacant land lot and camped for one year while building our dream home. We commuted together to work every day in order to save gas, and while my husband drove I was on the phone with subcontractors, scheduling for the next day.

   The laundry was put into plastic bags and we would have "Laundry Saturdays" at the Laundromat in town—just one sacrifice in a list of many. But it all paid off. We have been in our new home for almost a year now and we love it. We are still ahead of the curve even though real estate has fallen by about 25% in our area. Our son will graduate high school in two years, our daughter in four years, and our younger daughter in five years. We anticipate that at that time or before we will be ready to sell again and do what it says in the book—invest back into real estate by buying one or two rental properties.

We've grown to love real estate so much that I went to school and became an agent. I have been growing my business for a year now, even in this soft market. My husband is currently studying but will probably not make a move for a while so that I can continue to build up my business. I love real estate! Thank you so much for your book, David. There are all sorts of underlined and highlighted parts I am going to share with my clients, family, and coworkers.

—MICHELLE HANEY

ACKNOWLEDGMENTS

To everyone who has helped FinishRich Media and me help others live and finish rich, I say a heartfelt and humble THANK YOU!

The Automatic Millionaire Homeowner is the eighth book I've written in the FinishRich Series® in the last eight years. There are currently more than 4 million FinishRich books in print, translated into fifteen languages in more than forty countries. As our message spreads around the world, it is important to point out that I couldn't possibly have done this by myself. It takes a great team of great people to make a difference—and what follows is only a partial list of the many people who have helped us help others.

First, to my loyal readers—you really are why I do what I do. Your success energizes me and our team at FinishRich Media to wake up every day and help you to live a great life. To those of you who have sent us letters, e mails, and notes, come to our seminars or attended our coaching programs, and helped share the message, "Thank you, thank you, thank you." We will keep working hard to answer your questions and give you what you need to live and finish rich.

To my team at FinishRich Media, which is growing every day, thank you for working so hard to spread our mission. To Nicola Zahn, Unity Stoakes, Stephanie Oakes, Liz Dougherty, Susan Zimmerman, Andy DiSimone, Gabriella Weiser—you make coming to work fun. To Nicola Zahn—what can I say? You've travelled to more than sixty cities with me in less than a year, and you still smile at me! Thank you for keeping my life sane, my projects organized, and my spirits high. You are as wonderful to work with as anyone I have ever met and I feel blessed on a daily basis that you came into my life.

To my team outside FinishRich Media, thank you!

To my team at Doubleday Canada—thank you. To Maya Mavjec, Brad Martin, Stephanie Gowan, Valerie Gow, Bruce McDougall, Amy Black, Christine Innes, and Carla Kean—I appreciate all your work.

To Allan Mayer—we've now done six books together. This one was harder than most, yet you made it all seem easy. You are as good as they come and a total joy to work with. Your suggestions and edits and overall guidance in shaping this book (especially the 10,000 words you cut) made it what it is. Thank you—I really consider ours a world-class partnership.

To Jan Miller and Shannon Miser Marvin—thank you for what is now nearly a decade of representing me through the thick and thin of the publishing world. Your guidance has been immeasurable. Your promises have all come true. I both admire and love you ladies.

To Stephen Breimer—what a year we've had. Thank you for saying "no" when I wanted to say "yes"—and for protecting me on deal after deal. You are as good as they come in the legal profession, and as good as they come as a person. Thank you!

To my team at Doubleday Broadway Group—I love you guys. Most authors go from publisher to publisher. I've stayed with you since 1997, and I'm grateful that I have. You've worked diligently to grow my brand and protect its quality and integrity. To Kris Puopolo—you are a dream editor, and I know it! I sing your praises every day because I know your feedback is invaluable, brilliant—and right. Thank you for truly being both dedicated and interested in my books, their mission, and their message. You are my best reader—and because of that our readers are blessed. To my publisher, Stephen Rubin—I feel lucky to have the direct honest relationship we have. You make publishing enjoyable. To David Drake—gosh, eight books and counting. Who would have believed one could have a publicist for nearly a decade! You are just incredible. This will be our biggest book yet. To the sales and publishing team at Doubleday Broadway Group—Michael Palgon, Janelle Moburg, Janet Cooke, and so many more—you do the work that makes it all happen. To Catherine Pollack and Judy Jacoby, thank you for your brilliant guidance on marketing and advertising. To Jean Traina, thanks for making this cover fantastic and for listening patiently to all my suggestions and changes. I love the results!

To my family and friends—I'm officially apologizing. I'm sorry that my life has become so busy that I rarely see you, but I hope you know I love you! Thank you for continuing to call me, e-mail me, join me on the road—and visit me in New York. I miss you more than you know. To Mom and Dad (Bobbi and Marty Bach), the parents of all parents—you are just the best! No kid could be luckier. To my little sis, Emily—I love you!

To our sponsors of *The Great American Homeowner Challenge*™— in particular, Wells Fargo Home Mortgage, which came to the table first and said, "We want to help you reach 10 million people"—THANK YOU! A special "thank you" to Nancy Brennan, Cara Heiden, and Lisa Zakrajsek for carrying the torch to the "starting line." Our mission in 2006 is to empower those millions of people and I'm so excited that we'll be working together.

To our team at Yahoo—thank you for our partnership on *The Automatic Millionaire* column. What a blast it is to share our message with the world every two weeks through your platform.

To my wife, Michelle, and my two-year-old son, Jack—I love you so much! Jack, I promise that your daddy will be hanging with you at the park this year. Michelle, I'm really sorry. I promised you that after a year on the road I would spend the summer with you at the beach and relax, and instead I spent much of it in the library writing this book. Thank you for understanding. I promise to spend *this* summer at the beach with you and not in the library on book number nine.

Finally, to YOU reading this book—while we have not yet met personally I feel like I know you, and I thank you for being interested in my message of hope and prosperity and my mission to make a difference. I'm so grateful that you gave me the chance to be your coach, and I hope that we do get to meet face to face someday along the journey.

Live Rich,
David Bach
New York
November 2005

INDEX

ABOUT DAVID BACH

David Bach has helped millions of people around the world take action to live and finish rich. He is the author of seven consecutive national bestsellers, including two consecutive #1 *New York Times* bestsellers, *Start Late, Finish Rich* and *The Automatic Millionaire*, as well as the national and international bestsellers *Smart Women Finish Rich, Smart Couples Finish Rich, The Finish Rich Workbook,* and *The Automatic Millionaire Workbook.* Bach carries the unique distinction of having had four of his books appear simultaneously on the *Wall Street Journal, BusinessWeek,* and *USA Today* bestseller lists. In addition, four of Bach's books were named to *USA Today*'s Best Sellers of the Year list for 2004. In all, his FinishRich Books have been published in more than fifteen languages, with more than four million copies in print worldwide.

Bach's breakout book *The Automatic Millionaire* was the #1 Business book of 2004, according to *BusinessWeek.* It spent fourteen weeks on the *New York Times* bestseller list and was simultaneously number one on the bestseller lists of the *New York Times, BusinessWeek, USA Today,* and the *Wall Street Journal.* With over a million copies in print, this simple powerful book has been translated into twelve languages and has inspired thousands around the world to save money automatically.

Bach is also the author of *1001 Financial Words You Need to Know: The Ultimate Guide to the Language of Business and Finance*, published by Oxford University Press.

Bach is regularly featured on television and radio as well as in newspapers and magazines. He has appeared twice on *The Oprah Winfrey Show* to share his strategies for living and finishing rich. He has been a regular contributor to CNN's *American Morning* and has appeared frequently on ABC's *The View*, NBC's *Today* and *Weekend Today* shows, CBS's *Early Show*, Fox News Channel's *The O'Reilly Factor*, CNBC's *Power Lunch*, CNNfn, and MSNBC and *The Big Idea with Donny Deutsch*. He has been profiled in numerous major publications, including *The New York Times*, *BusinessWeek*, *USA Today*, *People*, *Reader's Digest*, *Time*, *Financial Times*, the *Washington Post*, the *Wall Street Journal*, *Los Angeles Times*, *San Francisco Chronicle*, *Working Woman*, *Glamour*, *Redbook*, and *Family Circle*. He is a featured contributor and columnist at Yahoo!, where his column "The Automatic Millionaire with David Bach" appears biweekly.

David Bach is the creator of the FinishRich® Seminar series, which highlights his quick and easy-to-follow financial strategies. In just the last few years, more than half a million people have learned how to take financial action to live a life in line with their values by attending his Smart Women Finish Rich®, Smart Couples Finish Rich®, and Find the Money Seminars, which have been taught in more than 2,000 cities throughout North America by thousands of financial advisors.

A renowned financial speaker, Bach regularly presents seminars for and delivers keynote addresses to the world's leading financial service firms, Fortune 500 companies, universities, and national conferences. He is the founder and Chairman of FinishRich Media, a company dedicated to revolutionizing the way people learn about money. Prior to founding FinishRich Media, he was a senior vice president of Morgan Stanley and a partner of The Bach Group, which during his tenure (1993 to 2001) managed more than half a billion dollars for individual investors.

David Bach lives with his wife, Michelle, and son, Jack, in New York, where he is currently working on his ninth book, *Go Green, Finish Rich* which will inspire people around the world to take action to protect the planet and get rich trying. Please visit his website at **www.finishrich.com**.

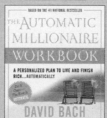
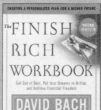

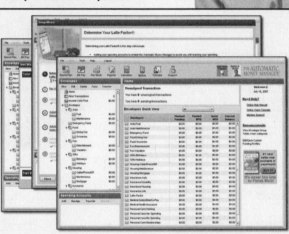